*The*
*Garland Library*
*of*
*War and Peace*

# The
# Garland Library
# of
# War and Peace

Under the General Editorship of
Blanche Wiesen Cook, *John Jay College,* C.U.N.Y.
Sandi E. Cooper, *Richmond College,* C.U.N.Y.
Charles Chatfield, *Wittenberg University*

# The War for Peace

by

**Leonard Woolf**

with a new introduction
for the Garland Edition by

Stephen J. Stearns

*Garland Publishing, Inc., New York & London*
1972

**Library of Congress Cataloging in Publication Data**

Woolf, Leonard Sidney, 1880-1969.
  The war for peace.

  (Garland library of war and peace)
  Reprint of the 1940 ed.
  1. Peace. 2. International relations. 3. Inter-
national cooperation. 4. Security, International.
I. Title. II. Series.
JX1952.W62 1972       327'.17       75-148376
ISBN 0-8240-0465-5

# Introduction

*War, that monster of human fratricide, will inevitably be wiped out by man's special progress and this will come about in the near future. But there is only one way to do it — war against war.*

Mao Tse Tung Strategic Problems of China's
Revolutionary War *(1935)*

*The winter of 1939-40 when Leonard Woolf wrote* The War for Peace *was probably among the grimmest he had known for a quarter of a century. For a half dozen years he had watched with horror the rise of the Nazi state, an epitome of the worst national savagery. In that autumn and winter he saw the beginning of the great European war which he had struggled to prevent since 1918 and the final ruin of the League of Nations which he had done so much to create. There followed the collaboration of the Soviet government in the partition of Poland and, even as he was at work writing his new book, their attack on Finland. All the hopeful arrangements worked out in 1918-19 to guarantee a safe and peaceful world had come to naught. Looking back on the interwar period years later, Woolf titled his autobiographical volume on those "low and dishonest decades" simply* Downhill All the Way.

Woolf's career in international relations had been devoted to the construction of a just, orderly and peaceful world under the rule of law. Born in 1880, he had graduated from Cambridge in 1904 and spent seven years in the Ceylon Civil Service. Disenchanted with his first-hand experience of imperialism he resigned during a home leave, married Virginia Stephen and devoted himself to nurturing her great but fragile genius while pursuing his own journalistic career. He attracted the attention of Sidney and Beatrice Webb before the First World War and was quickly recruited to write regularly for the New Statesman *and to work for the Fabians as an analyst of colonial and international affairs. During the war his reports on a postwar international organization, published as* International Government *(1916), had a significant influence on the planning which led to the creation of the League of Nations. After the war his books and articles won him a place as secretary of the Labour Advisory Committee on foreign policy and the empire. While his views commanded attention and respect, little was done to realize them. Lip service was paid to the importance of the role of the League in keeping international peace. In practice, however, it was ignored in the making of policy and regarded with suspicion by ministers and the Foreign Office alike. Even during the brief time that Labour was in power, in 1924 and again in 1929-31, Woolf had little success. The rise of the Nazis quickly convinced him that some kind of European war was inevitable. It was an unhappy conclusion but Woolf dutifully worked hard within the Labour party for the distasteful but necessary policy of rearmament to combat Nazism and Fascism. Though he had many friends among the Labour party's pacifists, he rejected the policy of their leader, George Lansbury, as sentimental.*

*In* The War for Peace *he wanted to make two key points. First he wanted to show that force was a legitimate instrument for peace-loving states and peoples to use – against aggressors. While this was paradoxical – that the road to peace was often blocked in such a way that only force could clear it – Woolf was a practical man. It was simply not a responsible position to leave the monopoly of force in the hands of the Nazis and Fascists. On the other hand, it was also clear that war was a very limited and negative instrument. All it could do was eliminate the challenge that the Nazis and Fascists posed to a peaceful world order. Their defeat would still leave the basic problem of how to construct a positive world order, in which force would be replaced by law and the arbitration of disputes, as far off as ever.*

*In 1940 there was not much argument in Britain about the necessity of combating the Nazis. There was precious little sentiment among British leadership for the alternative to war – making peace with the Nazis. Moreover, little thought or attention was paid to the prospects for the postwar world and the underlying, longer term problems — which caused the 1918 peace to fail.*

*On the eve of the second war, E.H. Carr's analysis of international relations from 1918 on,* The Twenty Years Crisis, *had launched a sustained attack on the lack of political realism, the shallow optimism and the vacuous idealism which had assumed that the existence of the League of Nations would solve the problem of war. Woolf's second point is an extended rejoinder to Carr and much of* The War for Peace *can only be understood in this context. Woolf was defending his conception of the League and the possibilities of resuscitating it after the war against Carr's attack.*

*Woolf's own thought about international relations was consistently grounded in a solid appreciation of the "cruel facts of life." However he remained optimistic in his belief that the nations of the world would be able to work out a stable, just and peaceful world order once they truly desired one. Time and again over his long career he made ample acknowledgment of the vicious and destructive human impulses which wracked society. He also saw that people had, over a long period of time, created something which they called civilization which acted to restrain their own barbarity. Journeying about London every day Woolf saw millions of people living peacefully, cheek by jowl, patiently "queuing" for the bus and looking after the flowers in their bits of back gardens. They were not systematically robbing*

INTRODUCTION

or killing each other. All of this activity was carried
on peacefully and without coercion. Was it not
possible, using the model of civil society, to conceive
that international society might be established in the
same peaceful fashion? Why wasn't it possible to have
the rule of civilized society — that is law — extended
over the relations between whole peoples, i.e., between their states? As Woolf clearly recognized,
among states as among people, there are violent
transgressors. These are in a minority in society, and
the majority act together to put down forcible
violation of the rules by using force themselves. What
is required to make such a system work is general
agreement on the rules and a general commitment to
their enforcement against transgressors. For Woolf
the place where agreement was worked out and the
instrument of enforcement was an active and forceful
League of Nations. The differences between Carr and
Woolf come down to whether or not such agreement
would ever be possible. Carr's position, looking back
at a century and a half of virulent nationalism, is that
states and people have competing interests, and that
in their relations their differences would prevail. The
notion that there might be a harmony of interests he
regarded as mere fatuity. The feeble character of the
League was its logical corollary.

Readers of The Twenty Years Crisis will be
impressed with the force and clarity that Carr brings
to bear against much of the genial fuzzymindedness
that prevailed in the interwar years. Woolf's posi-

9

*tion however and indeed his impatience with Carr's strictures against the supporters of the League, are not the complaints of a good man who has been told that he is a fool because he takes too sunny a view of human nature. Woolf was as aware as Carr that Bismarck, for example, had succeeded in unifying Germany, not by being reasonable, seeking accommodation and consensus, not by legal means, but by force. What Woolf questioned was why force should enjoy the sole claim of "political realism."*

*Woolf insisted on the correctness of the adage that those who live by the sword shall perish by it. From that it did not necessarily follow that human beings would be wise enough to give up force in resolving their differences. From his reading of the historical experience of the preceding 150 years Woolf could only insist that international relations based on "business-as-usual," laissez-faire, dog-eat-dog Darwinism, would lead to disaster. It had in 1914. It was doing so in 1940. It would do so again unless and until there was a general agreement among everyone that mutual slaughter must be eschewed. As Woolf well knew that time might never arrive and human civilization might well perish. Rather than accept doom passively he tried to point the way out of the abyss and toward survival. If people wanted to avoid wrecking human culture then they must learn to live without war. If they didn't care then we would all be doomed and that would be an end to it. But he rejected entirely the argument that a lemming-like*

# INTRODUCTION

*march to mutual ruin was "realism." To accept war as necessary or "inevitable" merely because of past failures to avoid it or because states were accustomed to using force, was for Woolf preposterous.*

*In 1916 Leonard Woolf had set out a model of* International Government. *(Vide reprint in the Garland Library of War and Peace, 1971.) Readers of that work will see that Woolf was one of the first in the twentieth century to comprehend the difficulties of adjusting relations between unequal groups of peoples and states. His arguments had not changed much, despite the unhappy experience of the intervening quarter century. He was throughout a man who stood for the necessity of taking the first reasonable steps toward that goal. We remain as hard-pressed as he was to devise institutional solutions to the problems of international anarchy and belligerence. Over the half century from* International Government, *through* The War for Peace *and to his death in 1969 no one can claim to have been any wiser than he was about the solution to those problems. Above all, he stood for the application of a humane intelligence to the organization of world peace and the necessary resistance to tyranny. We should honor his memory, respect his "realism," and struggle to realize his goals.*

S. J. Stearns
*Richmond College – C.U.N.Y.*

11

# THE WAR FOR PEACE

*By the same Author*

# HISTORY AND POLITICS

INTERNATIONAL GOVERNMENT
EMPIRE AND COMMERCE IN AFRICA
CO-OPERATION AND THE FUTURE OF INDUSTRY
SOCIALISM AND CO-OPERATION
FEAR AND POLITICS
IMPERIALISM AND CIVILIZATION
AFTER THE DELUGE. VOLS. I AND II.
QUACK, QUACK !
BARBARIANS AT THE GATE

# CRITICISM

HUNTING THE HIGHBROW
ESSAYS ON LITERATURE, HISTORY AND POLITICS

# FICTION

THE VILLAGE IN THE JUNGLE
STORIES OF THE EAST
THE WISE VIRGINS

# DRAMA

THE HOTEL

# THE WAR FOR PEACE

*By*

LEONARD WOOLF

LONDON

GEORGE ROUTLEDGE & SONS, LTD.

BROADWAY HOUSE : 68–74 CARTER LANE, E.C.4

*First published, 1940*

Printed in Great Britain by Butler & Tanner Ltd., Frome and London

# CONTENTS

| CHAP. | | PAGE |
|---|---|---|
| I | WAR . . . . . . . . . | 1 |
| II | POWER, INTERESTS, AND POLITICS . . . | 98 |
| III | PEACE . . . . . . . . | 184 |
| IV | A NOTE ON REASON . . . . . | 232 |

# THE WAR FOR PEACE

## CHAPTER I

# WAR

BETWEEN 1914 and 1918 the Great Powers of Europe fought what came to be known as the Great War, and before it ended the two Great Powers outside Europe, the United States of America and Japan, and most of the smaller states of the world had been drawn into it. A world war is a world war ; a world war means that all over the habitable globe, in Europe, in the Far East, in central Africa, and around the coasts of the two Americas, human beings kill or try to kill one another. That was, in plain and unadorned language, what people were doing or trying to do on a vast scale in 1918. It is to be presumed that they had, or thought they had, some object in doing so.

The war ended on November 11, 1918, and the world was once more at peace. Twenty-one years later another war broke out between those European Great Powers which had been the protagonist combatants of 1914 to 1918. It is not yet a world war, but it belongs to the category of great wars. This page is being written on the first day of the year 1940. To-day four out of five of the Great

## The War for Peace

Powers of Europe are at war ; at the other end of the world, in the Far East, Japan is engaged in a private war of her own, which involves 450,000,000 unfortunate inhabitants of China. Once more, therefore, hundreds of millions of the earth's population are engaged, with solemn concentration, in an organized effort to kill one another. The effort is meeting with considerable success, as it has done on previous occasions, and, since the human race is supposed to have a certain amount of reason and intelligence and to have attained a modest standard of civilization, one is forced to assume, at any rate on the first page of a book, that, as in 1914, those who are to-day engaged in this organized effort have, or think they have, an object in making it.

The statements in the last two paragraphs are platitudinous truisms. They sound a little silly. The bare truth, expressed in simple and homely language, such as a man is accustomed to use to his wife, his child, or his dog, nearly always sounds silly in politics and history, but it is none the less true. It is rarely thought of and never stated. The plain, unadorned truths which are the roots of politics and determine history get covered over by the complication of events, obscured by long words, resounding phrases, fierce emotions, the intricate criss-cross of human desires and objects, the cunning of the politician, and the ingenuity of learned theorists. They are nearly always forgotten until it is too late to remember them, but they continue to exist ; they are the stark, stupid realities which in the end mainly determine the success of those who remember and the failure of those who forget them.

This book is concerned with international relations and war and peace. It will have to deal with the complicated organization and practice of the relations between states, the tangled history of foreign policy, the fierce emotions of patriotism and nationalism, the intricate objects of national policy, the relation between power and national interests. All these things are relevant to the problem of war and peace, to the question, which is the main subject of this book, whether, when this war ends, it is or is not possible to regulate and organize the relations of Europeans and their states in such a way that periodic great wars become improbable. To-day and during the last twenty-five years the most important element in regulating those relations has been and is war. It is therefore necessary to start from this homely, if stupid, truth about war. War is to-day an organized effort by vast numbers of Europeans to kill one another, and it must be presumed that they have, or think they have, an object in doing this. The question which this book really tries to answer is : What is their object or what do they think it to be, and is war in fact a good method of attaining it ? The question is not a simple one ; it leads one far afield into history, politics, psychology, and even perhaps philosophy.

## The War for Peace

I am well aware that, like everyone else, I shall be again and again in danger of forgetting, during the argument, what war really is. That is why I wish, both for my own sake and for the sake of the reader, to insist upon this simple truth about the nature of war. Whatever be its cause or its object, it remains an organized effort by vast numbers of human beings to kill one another. Provided that we have got that firmly fixed in our mind, we are in a position to go on to consider whether such action is a necessary or appropriate method of regulating the relations of human beings, organized in nations or states. Let us begin by examining the nature of war a little more closely. War is the supreme instrument of national power, the means by which in the last resort a state tests its power in relation to other states or, in other words, whether it can impose its will upon them by force. The power of states in relation to one another depends upon a large number of different factors, e.g. size of population, extent of territory, geographical position in so far as that may give it strategical or economic advantages or disadvantages, its control of raw materials, the organization of its industries, the capacities and training of its citizens, and the efficiency of its government. The relative power of two states is simply the relative ability of each to impose its will upon the other by force or the threat of force. Suppose you have a state A with a government X and a state B with a government Y ;

4

then A is more powerful than B if X can compel
Y to do what X desires ; B is less powerful than A,
if Y cannot do what Y desires owing to X.

The power of one state may in certain circumstances be used hostilely with effect against another
without war. Before the war of 1914 the geographical position of Austria gave it considerable
power, mainly of an economic nature, over Serbia,
and the Austrian government used this economic
power on more than one occasion to compel the
Serbian government to do, against its own will,
the will of the Austrian government. But the
ultimate arbiter of national power in the world of
states, as we have known it for the last hundred
years, has been war, and behind the use of economic
power as an instrument of policy in peace has
always lain the threat of military force. This was
certainly the case as between Serbia and Austria ;
Austria's economic power over Serbia was always
exercised in peace, and was only effective, because
behind it was the threat of war, and the great war
actually began because the Austrian government
decided that the time had come when the threat
must be carried out and the final test of power
should be made in war. That particular case
shows another important fact about national power,
namely that it does not depend solely upon the
intrinsic possessions, position, qualities, etc., of a
state. Its potential power may also depend upon
alliances, and a state, like Serbia, which by itself

was unable to resist the will of Austria, may with the help of allies not only successfully resist, but destroy its more powerful opponent.

War is, then, the ultimate test or arbiter of national power as between states. It decides, or is intended to decide, which of two states is the stronger, i.e. which can impose its will upon the other by force. That does not alter the fact which was stated in the first paragraphs of this book, and which the reader, I hope, will keep in his mind until the book ends, the fact that war is an organized effort of human beings to kill one another in large numbers. On the contrary, the one fact is the corollary of the other. A state is not a person, though metaphorically we all speak of it as such and some deluded people have even believed that some mystic personality attaches to states. A state is a group or association of separate persons, inhabiting a certain defined territory, united under a common government. A state, as compared with a person, is an abstraction—no one has ever seen, touched, smelt, or tasted a state ; no one has ever heard a state speaking, even out of the thunder on Mount Sinai or on the radio. A state cannot therefore bring its power or force to bear directly on another state, nor can the " government " of a state exercise power or force directly against the " government " of another state. For political purposes power can only be used against individuals and force can only be made operative or effective against individuals. A state has no power, no force, and no will except metaphorically ; in the world of real life its power, force, and will can only be applied by individuals against individuals.

When, therefore, we speak of the power of one state being greater than that of another or of the power of one state being used to compel another state to do this or that or not to do this or that, we mean in the last resort that certain individuals in state A are able to take certain action which effectively compels certain individuals in state B to do this or not to do that. Power is always applied by individuals to individuals ; there are many different ways of exercising it, but there is a family likeness in most forms of force. The more powerful man confronts the weaker man with some form of physical force and a choice of evils, the least of the evils being, *ex hypothesi*, to yield to the will of the stronger. In societies in which the use of sheer physical force by individuals has not been regulated and circumscribed, the strong man uses his power over the weak man by compelling him to choose between death, torture, or beating and doing what the strong man wants. If you hear a noise downstairs in the middle of the night and, on investigation, find yourself confronted in your dining-room by a burglar holding your silver spoons in one hand and a revolver in the other, his power is exercised by confronting you with a choice between being shot and letting him escape with your spoons. In more civilized societies, power is often exercised in accordance with the laws of economics rather than ballistics, and the individual in an economically strong position may force his weaker brother to work for a certain wage by confronting him with a choice between starvation and doing what the strong man asks him to do. In all these cases the weaker individual may resist and then the actual force may be applied—then there will be killing, beating, or starving.

A state or a government cannot be killed, beaten, or starved ; it is individuals, citizens of the state, or members of the government, who can be killed, beaten, or starved. Or they may be imprisoned or put into concentration camps or made to drink castor oil—but no one has ever tried to imprison a state or dose it with castor oil. It is, therefore, only metaphorically that we can say that a state has power or can exercise power ; what we really mean when we say that a state like Germany is more powerful than Poland, or Italy than Albania, or Britain than the Transvaal, is that the inhabitants of a certain area of territory, owing to the possession of certain advantages, such as numbers or strategical position or arms or control of raw materials or the development of their industry or agriculture, can compel the inhabitants of the other area of territory by force to do what they want them to do. National policy is what the inhabitants of a state want to do, or more usually what their government wants

8

to do in their name, in relation to the inhabitants of other states ; it is the political objective or purpose which the individuals inhabiting a particular area of territory pursue in their relations with individuals outside that territory. The connection of power with policy is, therefore, of the utmost importance. Power policy, as it is called, or the use of power as an instrument of national policy, means that the individuals inhabiting a certain territory use their power *against* the individuals outside their territory in order to achieve by force their purpose or objective.

Many people will think that in the previous paragraph I am still uselessly announcing obvious platitudes and irrelevant truisms. On the contrary, these are by far the most important and relevant, and most neglected, truths about policy and international relations. They are the real facts which lie behind history and war and peace ; they will probably decide the fate of civilization and may determine whether you who read this sentence live to old age and die in your bed or are needlessly blown to pieces in youth by a high explosive shell. If the governments and the doomed citizens of these fictitious " Great Powers " really understood these facts and kept them steadily before their minds when they thought and talked about " international policy ", they would cease to believe nearly all the deadly nonsense and fairy tales which now determine the relations of sovereign states, questions of

9

war and peace, and the future of civilization. And if learned writers on history and politics would do the same, they would not only turn a great deal of rubbish out of their own minds and books, but might cease to spin out of the same deadly nonsense and fairy tales the cleverest theories to support or rationalize our social savagery and political stupidity.

These childish and elementary facts about states, individuals, power, force, and policy are peculiarly relevant if you are considering the problem of war and international relations, the question whether war is a necessary element in human society. War is the ultimate instrument of national policy when that policy is based upon power. War breaks out when, to use the inaccurate language in which we normally talk about politics, a state decides to impose its policy upon another, if necessary, by force, and the other decides to resist. Translated into the world of facts and reality this means that a large number of individuals inhabiting a certain area have to use such power as they possess individually and collectively to compel a large number of individuals in another area to do what they do not want to do. The exercise of power by an individual against an individual or by a few individuals against a few individuals in immediate contact with one another is a comparatively simple matter. The question who is the stronger can be settled on the spot by physical force, if there is resistance on one side or the other, and the instruments of effective power are beating, torturing, imprisonment, or in the last resort killing. But for enormous numbers of individuals to exercise power, individually and collectively, against enormous numbers of individuals hundreds or thousands of miles away is a much more complicated business. Germany cannot beat, torture, imprison, or kill Britain, and in fact 78,000,000 Germans living in Germany cannot beat, imprison, or kill 46,000,000 Britons living in England, Scotland, and Wales. The exercise of direct physical violence by the government against the government, e.g. by Adolf Hitler against Neville Chamberlain, is also not feasible,[1] or at least has not so far been accepted as a method of settling international disputes by force. The ingenuity of man has therefore devised war and gradually elaborated the complicated system of modern war by which national groups of individuals can test their power and so regulate their differences by force.

Modern war is extremely complicated, but all

---

[1] It is worth remarking that in the old days, when rule was more personal than it has been until recent years, attempts were often made to exercise national power by personal acts of violence against the rulers, i.e. the government. Kings were captured, imprisoned, even beaten and tortured, by their adversaries, and one might almost say with accuracy that in such cases power and force were used directly by a government against a government. Even in the nineteenth century Napoleon kidnapped and held prisoner the king of Spain. It is significant that quite recently there have been signs of a return to this method of exercising national power. The way in which Hitler treated Herr Schuschnigg and other heads of neighbouring states upon which he wished to impose his will recalls the methods of pre-nineteenth-century Europe.

war merely adapts to large numbers of individuals
the ordinary methods of using power or force against
a single individual or a few individuals. This is
inevitable because the ways in which power can be
exerted and force used are strictly limited. In the
playground of any school you may watch a large
boy exert his power over a small boy by methods
which were certainly used in the same way and
for similar purposes by our ancestors in the Stone
Age. It was my duty at one time as a representative
of His Majesty King Edward VII to stand in a
prison courtyard and see that a sentence of flogging
was duly executed upon a prisoner or that a con-
demned murderer was hanged by the neck until
he was dead. The scene was in Asia, the period
the twentieth century A.D., the time an early tropical
morning before breakfast, which was always chosen
for these ceremonies. As I stood with the Superintendent of the Prison, who came from Wormwood
Scrubbs, the Superintendent of Police, who came
from Repton, and the Medical Officer, who came
from Edinburgh, with the mountains towering up
into the clear sky above the prison walls, the
representative of the " power of the state " and of
" the force of society "—inappropriately dressed in
a white suit and a sun-helmet—who had come to
see that the ultimate instruments of that social
power and force should be used in due form against
an individual, I was aware that 3,800 years ago, not
so very far away beyond the mountains in the

valley of the great Asiatic rivers, the bearded
representatives of Hammurabi, Emperor of Sumer
and Akkad, had watched the power of the state
and the force of society executed in precisely the
same way and by the same methods against the
recalcitrant individual. And to-day in Europe,
when a Hitler in Germany, a Mussolini in Italy,
or a Stalin in Russia sets up a dictatorship, which
is a personal or oligarchic government based upon
power and force, they may call it fascism, national-
socialism, or communism, but the methods by which
they establish and maintain their power, use their
force, and impose their will—the executions, purges,
liquidations, imprisonments, beatings, castor oil,
concentration camps, and forced labour—are the
same which all dictators have been compelled to
use from the time of Melchisidek to the year 1940.

These facts apply to interstate relations no less
than to relations between individuals and between
governments and their own citizens. They set
narrow limits to the way in which the " power of
a state " can be exercised against another, if it is
no longer a question of threats, but of the use of
force and physical violence. Power, as we have
seen, can only be exercised upon individuals, and,
if it comes actually to the use of force, only by
confronting individuals physically with a choice of
evils. War is only the necessary adaptation of these
facts to the use of power and force by large masses
of men against large masses of men. The power

of an individual A is operative and successful
against an individual B, when A is able to force
B to do unwillingly what A wants him to do,
because B would rather do that than suffer some
physical evil, such as pain, imprisonment, hunger,
or death which A can inflict on him. Under
similar circumstances, a large number of individuals,
whom we personify as a state, can only impose their
will upon another large number of individuals,
whom we personify as another state, if the first can
force the second to do what they want, because the
second group would rather do this than suffer the
physical evils which the first group is able to inflict
upon them. Experience has proved that death is
a physical evil which most human beings will do
almost anything to avoid. Imprisonment, beating,
torture, starvation are all excellent and well-tried
instruments of power, effective varieties of force,
but, when all is said and done, there is nothing
like death.

The efficacy of killing and death as forms of force
and therefore as instruments of power has determined the nature of war, which is the instrument
of national power. War has a long history and has
changed its superficial characteristics from age to
age, in accordance with the changes in men's way
of life and the weapons which they have devised
for killing one another. It has always used and still
uses the lesser forms of misery through which power
is made effective and groups of individuals may be

forced to do what they do not want to do. Starvation, for instance, has always been a pretty good instrument of national power. If the individuals inhabiting Great Britain, owing to geographical position, possession of ships, and some other things, are able to inflict starvation or semi-starvation upon the individuals inhabiting Germany, the former will probably be able to impose their will on the latter and " Great Britain " will then have proved herself a more powerful state than " Germany ". But the trouble about starvation and other similar forms of force is that they lead almost logically and inevitably to killing, simply because in a world ordered by force death is king. The starving will resist the starvers by every means in their power, and to kill your opponent is the most convincing form of resistance. Also the starver says to the starved : " If you don't do what I want, I shall starve you, and if you won't be starved, well, I must kill you." And further, where you have large numbers of individuals attempting in the name of states or nations to apply force to one another, killing is extraordinarily effective, or at first sight appears to be so ; by killing enough individuals on the other side you may put the fear of death into the survivors so that they will do what you want in order to escape being killed. So that from whatever side you start in this system of national power, force, and war, you get back to death and killing.

These are the causes which determine the nature

of war and of modern war, which make it an organized effort of individuals, divided into groups, to kill one another on a large scale. The scale has varied in different ages and that is an important fact, for it is only in recent times that the scale of the killing has become enormous. Man is a strange animal—as we all know, there is nothing like him in the whole animal kingdom. He suffers from a divided mind and a divided soul—if, indeed, he has a soul. His eyes are uplifted to the stars while his feet stumble over molehills into cesspools. If you tune into the B.B.C. Home Service, you will learn that he has an inexhaustible appetite for clean fun, purity, beauty, reason, knowledge, the Royal Family, and truth. If you listen to your friends' conversation, examine your own mind, and study history, you will learn that he is also a nasty, dirty, cunning, treacherous, ignorant, superstitious, savage, stupid biped. This dichotomy of the human being makes his behaviour, particularly his collective behaviour, peculiarly erratic and unpredictable. It is complicated by the fact that the human race has been cursed with the possession not only of reason, which it very rarely uses, but of a curious form of imbecile mental action which we call imagination, and which it is apt to use in unexpected ways and at unexpected moments.

The human imagination has always been accustomed to get to work in curious ways where there was collective action by groups of individuals for a common purpose. The imagination frequently works by turning the collective action into a kind of game or ritual with elaborate rules and ceremonies, which often conceal or frustrate the real purpose of the collective action. Indeed, tribes, nations, and other groups commonly go on performing certain actions for centuries after their original purpose has been forgotten, mainly because that purpose has been smothered by the ceremony or ritual, the game of the imagination. Thus they went on killing kings long after they had forgotten that the real reason why you kill your king is to make the crops grow. War, or the use of collective power or force by tribal and national groups against one another, did not escape the influence of this peculiar form of imagination during the long periods of history which preceded the nineteenth century. At times it became little more than a dangerous and brutal game and it was almost always overlaid with a complicated ceremonial or ritual. Its original and ultimate purpose, the compulsion of one group of individuals by another, was perhaps never completely forgotten, and killing or the threat of death as the most effective method of compulsion has always remained its most marked characteristic, for human beings have never discovered a more efficient instrument of individual or collective coercion than death. But they contrived to turn the killing itself into the most elaborate games and ritual. There have been times and places in which tribal warfare has practically ceased to be a test of tribal power, and its original object, to obtain your neighbour's land, women, or cattle by killing him, became of secondary importance. The hunting of heads became a game or ceremony pursued for its own sake and head-hunting a specialized occupation. When that happens, the head-hunters develop into an aristocracy and war becomes a vested interest.

In later and more sophisticated ages much the same kind of thing has happened. It has been an almost universal custom to entrust the killing of individuals belonging to a national group which it is desired to coerce to a specialized class and war was an organized effort by these warrior or combatant classes to kill one another. It was both a vested interest of the professional soldier and a game or ritual with artificial conventions and elaborate rules.[1] The original purpose of war was never completely forgotten. It was almost always waged for a definite purpose and was a test of national power, an attempt by one national group to impose its purpose upon another by making life so unbearable to a sufficient number of individuals in the hostile group that they would, as we say, " give in ". The killing of non-combatants, the destruction of crops, the sacking or starving of cities have therefore always remained legitimate methods of warfare (provided they were

[1] That this is still the case is shown by the persistence of " rules " or even " laws " of war which prescribe in what ways or with what weapons it is or is not legitimate to kill soldiers.

done according to rule) and have been used again and again as primary instruments of national power, the purpose being for one group of individuals to impose its will by using its power of making life unbearable to another group. But the task of making life unbearable, the main military operations, were confined to specialized " combatants ", to highly trained armies commanded by professional soldiers. It was here that the human imagination got to work with astonishing results. The main duty of armies in war is to destroy one another. This became an end in itself to the professional soldier, a strange mixture of game, art, ritual, and religious ceremony. Immense labour and ingenuity were given to elaborating rules, tactics, and strategy, to drilling and training bodies of men, to inventing weapons. The successful head of an army acquired something very like divinity and that army itself became a religious body ; there was something sacramental in the colour of a regimental uniform. But perhaps the most astonishing thing about this transfiguration of the crude reality of war by human imagination is this, that the work of moving large bodies of individuals about in such a way that they can more easily kill one another has been transformed into one of the noblest of human sciences. Historians and philosophers have written learned and famous works to explain the subtleties and beauties of this science, and men who, in accordance with its principles, have proved exceptionally competent to manœuvre large bodies of men in such a way as to destroy large bodies of other men among the sands of Asia or the rivers of Germany are counted among the greatest geniuses and heroes produced by the human race.

We shall have to consider later on in this book a theory very popular at the present time among politicians and professors that there is something peculiarly " real " in power, force, and violence, and therefore in national power and its instrument, war, and that anyone who does not swallow the theory whole or who suggests that it might be possible to deal with national power in Europe by methods other than those of the head-hunters in Pacific Islands or even to prevent war by some such system as the League of Nations is a purblind utopian.

The facts given above about the nature of war before the nineteenth century are highly relevant to this theory and to the future problem of war and peace. They are again facts of such a simple and silly nature that one feels somewhat ashamed to mention them to politicians, historians, and practical men. Yet it is necessary to do so because, if there is such a thing as reality, it is to be found in the simple and silly facts, the bare and bleak truth. For these facts, which are practically never mentioned, suggest that the idea of something peculiarly " real " in national power and war is itself a delusion. They suggest that tribal or national power and war are, like most human activities or contrivances, a mixture of fact and fancy, of reality and romance, fairy tales, or game. The reality consists in the simple fact that if A (whether A is an individual or a group of individuals, called a nation) has the power to make life intolerable to B or to kill B, while B has not the same power with regard to A, then A, if he is allowed full exercise of that power, will in nine cases out of ten be able to make B do what he wants ; in the tenth case he will have either to give up the attempt or kill A, which will probably give him some satisfaction, but will not necessarily produce the same result as if B had chosen the alternative of remaining alive and obeying A. That is the reality. The romance comes in as soon as people begin to regard this power of making life intolerable or of killing as something fixed and immutable. It is nothing of the kind ; on the contrary, its effect, its very existence, depends upon men's attitude towards it, how they deal with it. Lightning is, no doubt, a reality, but there is no earthly or divine reason why you should not conduct a flash of lightning from a cloud to the earth through a lightning conductor rather than, with disastrous results to your house, through the chimney pot. Of course, if you believe that there is some peculiar reality attaching to lightning as the bolt or instrument with which God strikes the more than ordinarily great sinner, you will continue to allow divine vengeance to pursue its way effectively via the chimney pot rather than innocuously via the lightning conductor. But if you stick to the facts and leave it to the poets, the priests, and those who have a vested interest in thunder and divine vengeance to make a song about the lightning, you will soon find that there is no difficulty in controlling all three : the lightning, the divine vengeance, and the vested interests.

It is much the same with power and war. The romance comes in, as I said, when people begin to regard this power of killing and making life intolerable as a fixed and immutable element in human society. The second stage in the romance comes when the exercise of power, the making of life intolerable and the killing, become an end in themselves, a game, a ceremony, and a vested interest. That is what happened to war prior to the nineteenth century. It still remained and was frequently used as an instrument of national or tribal power, and was continually successful in killing or making life intolerable for immense numbers of human beings. As such an instrument, it frequently performed its purpose, i.e. national groups or governments were forced to do or accept things which they did not wish to do or accept. All kinds of things were in this way " settled " by war, e.g. that peoples should be ruled by rulers whom they did not like, that frontiers should be drawn here rather than there, that a certain prince should or should not marry a certain princess, that the inhabitants of one territory should believe in a certain divine truth and the inhabitants of another should believe in a contradictory divine truth.

But upon this primary or " real " function of war there were superimposed functions which were derived from the fairy-tale or nightmare world of men's imagination. It became a romance, a game, a ceremony, a profession, a religion, an art, a science, and a vested interest. The nature of this fairy tale or nightmare has varied from age to age. Perhaps the Middle Ages in Europe produced the most fantastic and unreal form which war has ever assumed. It became the monopoly occupation of a small upper class, a completely stylized and artificial ceremony, an elaborate game, and at the same time a vested interest ; its original function as an instrument of power practically ceased to exist and it is impossible to see that it retained any connection with any real social or human interest. And yet this mediæval view of war still colours the attitude of many Europeans, particularly in the " upper classes " and in armies, even to-day. It is therefore worth while studying the description of war in the Middle Ages given in the following quotation :

> The nobles of Europe led a life without precedent in the history of the world, and since they constituted the upper class, which the other classes took as their model, they initiated customs, and even sentiments, which have survived up to our own day. They lived on their domains among peasants who were their inferiors, and had no duty save that of war, learning

nothing but horsemanship and the profession of arms and spending their time mostly in riding, hunting, and making war, unable to read or write, yet accustomed to feeling superior owing to their rank and strength. They restored physical exercise and country life to honour. The nobleman's dwelling-place was a fortified house, or even a castle surrounded by a thick, high stone wall, flanked by towers at the corners and defended by a broad moat which could only be crossed when the drawbridge was lowered. The *castle*, the centre of defence and dominion, has remained the type of a dignified abode. In England, as early as the Middle Ages, the king forbade his subjects to make war upon one another, and the castles had ceased to be fortresses, so that gentlemen ceased to take up their knighthood or even to possess warlike weapons ; but the life of the castle, restricted to the peaceful occupations of riding and hunting, has continued to be the life of a privileged class. It has survived as the permanent characteristic of the nobility in every country of Europe.

War was regarded by the nobles not as a misfortune, but as a pleasure, and even as an opportunity of obtaining wealth by pillaging an enemy's domain or taking him prisoner and holding him to ransom. A substitute for war was sometimes found by arranging in advance for a combat between the nobles of one and the same country. This was the original form of the *tournament*, in which both sides fought with warlike weapons, taking prisoner those whom they unhorsed and holding them to ransom.[1]

Note that the nobles of Europe " had no duty save that of war ", that " war was regarded by " them " not as a misfortune, but as a pleasure, and even as an opportunity of obtaining wealth by

[1] *The Rise of European Civilization*, by Charles Seignobos.

pillaging an enemy's domain or taking him prisoner and holding him to ransom ", that the life of the " castle " or fortified house of the warrior has continued " to be the life of a privileged class " and " has survived as the permanent characteristic of the nobility in every country of Europe ". Until the nineteenth century society in every country of Europe was aristocratic ; the form and colour of life were determined for all classes by the political and economic power of the nobles, and therefore by aristocratic psychology and interests. War was naturally one of the social activities which were subjected to these influences throughout the period which separated the Middle Ages from the industrial revolution. It remained the " sport of kings " and an elaborate game of the upper classes in which the prizes were honours and profit.[1] It is true that the gradual evolution of the national state, as we now know it, had an immediate effect upon the nature of war ; it came to be used more and more as an instrument of national power. But until the end of the eighteenth century this " real " function was combined with its artificial function of being a game or occupation for the upper classes. Even in the eighteenth century wars were still limited and stylized operations which on the whole could be carried on without much disturbance of life to

[1] These ideas persist to-day in the almost universal rule that the actual conduct of war must be a monopoly of the upper classes, that " officers " must be gentlemen, and that normally the lower classes should not rise above the rank of sergeant-major.

large numbers of the population. They were fought on frontiers, as a rule, with no great numbers of troops ; the troops themselves were often foreign mercenaries, paid professionals, who may be compared with the modern professional football player ; invasions or battles on a large scale were extremely rare, and operations were slow, laborious, ceremonial, and consisted largely of elaborate sieges which, whether successful or unsuccessful, had no decisive effect upon the course of the war.

The evolution of the modern national state, as was noted above, had an immediate effect upon the nature of war, but its full effect was only made possible by the industrial revolution and the birth of Napoleon Bonaparte. Napoleon was a genius ; he was one of those men to whom the human race accords the greatest admiration and the highest honour, for his genius consisted largely in a superhuman ability to move large masses of men about in fields, over roads, across rivers and mountains, in such a way that they were infallibly brought into positions in which they could destroy other large masses of men. Thousands of books, of the most learned and technical nature, have been written regarding Napoleon's methods of doing this, and the splendour of his science or art of destroying large bodies of human beings dressed up in uniform has received far higher praise than that of a Newton or a Michelangelo. When dictators and professors preach to us about the peculiar " reality " in national

power and force and war and about the " unreality "
of peace and the League of Nations, it is sometimes
salutary to recall these facts. It depends entirely
upon what exactly one means by reality. Reality
appears to be one thing to the inhabitants of a
lunatic asylum, some of whom are probably convinced that they are Jesus Christ and others Julius
Ceasar ; it is quite different to the man outside,
who is perhaps digging his garden, pruning his apple
trees, or sowing cabbage seeds. I believe that most
people outside lunatic asylums—some of which are
built of bricks and mortar and others of ideas—if
they would for a moment look at Napoleon and his
activities in the cold light of truth rather than the
limelight of melodramatic romance which is called
history and political science, would see that the
reality of Napoleon's world is the reality of the
lunatic asylum, where John Smith is not John Smith
but Jesus Christ and Tom Jones is not Tom Jones
but Julius Cæsar, that Napoleon's occupations and
activities were part of a dream or game which
became actual only because we dream the dreams
and play the games of lunatics, and that there is
more reality, more utility, and more glory in the
occupation of a man sowing a threepenny packet of
cabbage seed in his back garden than in that of a
man winning the great battle of Austerlitz.

Napoleon was not only a curse to Europe while
he lived ; the evil that he did lived after him. He
contrived, with the help of nationalism and the

industrial revolution, to alter the nature of European war. Hitherto, as we have seen, it had been employed only in part and half-heartedly as an instrument of power ; it was always regarded by kings and aristocratic governments in part as a game, a ritual, and a profession. Its effects were always limited, and it was a limited social curse or evil. After Napoleon it became a universal catastrophe, threatening to involve all nations, the whole of each nation, and all classes in the nation. The change actually began to take place before Napoleon ; you can see it beginning in the form and strategy of the first revolutionary armies of France which drove back the invading troops of the allied Powers into Belgium. These revolutionary armies fought for an idea, and that idea was really the French revolution and the French republic ; they fought, not as the aristocratic armies of the eighteenth century fought, according to the rules of a game, but in order to impose their will upon the other side. Their behaviour and tactics and strategy outraged the Duke of Brunswick and the allied commanders, for they did not " play the game " ; for instance, when beaten they did not retreat, but attacked again and again.

Napoleon carried this process of development to its logical conclusion. By conscription he turned the army into the nation and the nation into the army. And he used his armies, not for the purposes of a game or according to the rules of a game,

but as instruments of power ; he used them in order
to impose the will of France or rather of Napoleon
—for Napoleon was France—upon other nations.
This object determined his strategy.

> Napoleon had grasped a fact which professional
> soldiers had not clearly realized : that war is not an
> end in itself. It is merely a means of forcing the
> enemy to accept the policy which it is desired to
> impose upon him, by occupying his territory and
> destroying his armies. War as he waged it was not
> that of the eighteenth century, that is to say, it was
> neither siege-warfare nor a war of positions. His
> method was a rapid invasion, making use of surprise,
> so as to arrive at a decisive battle in which he would
> have the superiority of numbers." [1]

Napoleonic war is in embryo the totalitarian **war**
which we enjoy to-day. All through the nineteenth
century the process which Napoleon began went
on until it developed into the full totalitarian war
of the dictators. The enormous development of
industry and science, the vast increase in population,
and conscription made it possible to turn the whole
nation into a tremendous instrument of power, and
the violent emotions of patriotism and nationalism
enabled governments to use the armed nation as
their instrument of national policy. This changed
the nature of war. It ceased to be an end in itself,
a game, or a social activity limited to certain classes
in the population ; it involved the whole nation
and every individual in it, and it was inevitable

[1] *The Rise of European Civilization,* by Charles Seignobos.

that sooner or later the distinction between combatant and non-combatant must disappear, just as the professional army disappeared.

This evolution of nineteenth-century warfare had two important results. In the first place it became much more dangerous to the stability of states, of Europe, and of civilization. When war was the sport of kings and a pastime for the idle and noble rich, it was fought with limited objectives and with a minimum of inconvenience to the rest of the population. It was unpleasant to be in a beleaguered city, and the property and chastity of the bourgeoisie, not to speak of the lower orders, might be in danger if the siege were successful. But even in a long war the majority of the population who did not live on the frontiers of the belligerent nations were often very little affected by it. And because wars were fought for limited and usually unimportant objectives, they did not disturb the bases of national or European society. There was fighting in Europe all through the eighteenth century and all the great Powers were at one time or another at war. But at no time was the national existence of any of these Powers threatened by war, and no one in that century could possibly feel that war might result in social revolution or the break up of civilization. Napoleon and the nineteenth century changed all that. As soon as war began really to be used as an instrument of national power and the whole of one nation was mobilized to exert force upon

another, the thing became much more serious, for
every class and every individual in the nation was
involved and the results of defeat might be catas-
trophic. War immediately became a menace to
national and international society and to civilization
itself, for, if it once broke out, it was extremely
difficult to localize or to limit it. The danger was
enormously increased by the progress in human
science which led to the invention of weapons of
incredibly destructive power, by which it has become
possible to kill human beings on a scale and in
numbers which our ancestors would have regarded
as utopian. In the twentieth century every war,
once it has broken out, no matter what its cause
was originally, is a war for " national existence " ;
for that reason it is fought with the utmost ruthlessness ; it is always likely to extend its area and
develop into a " world war ", and its effects are
so devastating upon the closely knit world society
of our day that they may be just as disastrous,
economically and socially, to the neutrals as to
the belligerents.

It is interesting to see that keen-sighted men
noted this change taking place in the nature of war
and in its effects on human society at the very
beginning of the process, and long before it had
fully established itself. There is a passage in
Guizot's *Mémoires de mon Temps* (Vol. IV, Chapter
22) in which, dealing with the years 1832 to 1836,
he insists that the pacific foreign policy of the king,

Louis-Philippe, was a necessity for France and for Europe and that those who attacked it and wanted France to assert herself in Europe, even at the risk of war, were heading for disaster, because they ignored " realities " in modern war and the modern world.

> A policy of war and conquest, [he writes] formerly did not have the consequences which it has to-day ; everywhere in Europe it encountered obstacles, counterbalances, limitations ; its breath was not a universal hurricane ; the most ambitious enterprises of Charles V and of Louis XIV did not imperil all the states of Europe or shake the foundations of human society. A term could be and was in fact set to them, or rather a limit was set both to their success and to their designs. To-day Europe is a great organism, with a unity and susceptibility which is quite different ; all vital questions are raised and ferment everywhere throughout its length and breadth ; every evil is contagious, every trouble becomes general. When some large enterprise is undertaken, no one can measure its effect nor can he be certain that he can stop himself once the impetus has been given. The problem always turns out to be vaster and more complicated than one has foreseen ; a blow struck in one corner makes the whole building tremble and a movement is always apt to develop into chaos.

Thus the evolution of nineteenth-century war has had a most dangerous effect upon the stability of the national state, upon the whole society of European states, and upon civilization itself. Its second important effect has been in the methods of warfare and their relation to the individual and to society.

## *War*

As was pointed out above, the methods by which power and force can be exercised against human beings and in human society are limited. The effective use of power means simply the ability of an individual or individuals to make the life of another individual so intolerable that the former can impose their will on the latter. This is true, no matter who the individual or individuals may be ; it is true of the husband who effectively beats his wife, of the employer who effectively breaks a strike, of the hooligan who holds up someone in a deserted street and robs him of his purse, of the state which fines, imprisons, hangs or beheads the hooligan, and of the nation which is victorious over another nation in war. There are, of course, a good many different ways in which it is possible to make people's lives unbearable, but even they are strictly limited : you can starve, hurt, beat, imprison, or in the last resort kill, but when you have said that, you have about exhausted the list ; the variety really comes in in the different ways in which you can starve, hurt, beat, imprison, and kill. The sovereign independent state is bound no less by the stern reality of the nature of force than is the strong husband or the armed hooligan ; it can impose its will and exercise its power only by starving, hurting, beating, imprisoning and killing. The evolution of the state and of warfare in the nineteenth century has not changed this ; it has only changed the methods and weapons by which it is possible to

33

make life intolerable or to destroy life, and therefore the scale of suffering and of killing.  But this
change is of some importance for those individuals
who have the privilege of being citizens of the
sovereign states of Europe.  War, as an instrument
of national power, is now an attempt by millions of
individuals to make life intolerable to or destroy
millions of other individuals.  Scientists, great
industrialists, and the passions of nationalism make
it possible for governments to attempt this successfully on a scale never before possible.  War is no
longer a rather dangerous and dirty game played
by professional soldiers with professional armies, and
the non-combatant is an anachronism.  It is an
attempt of millions to coerce millions, and since, as
we saw, where force reigns death is king, war has
become literally an organized effort of human beings
to kill one another on a gigantic scale.

Whether this is a reasonable and necessary method
of regulating human affairs, and in particular the
relations between the inhabitants of the various
countries of Europe, is a question which will be
discussed further in these pages.  But before doing
so it is advisable to remind the reader of another
aspect of war.  It may be, as so many people now
tell us, that power, force, and war are ultimate
" realities " in human society and that any attempt
to control or abolish them from international society
is utopian, that international relations must always
be determined by power and therefore ultimately

34

by the threat or use of force in the shape of war. If so, then indubitably civilization is utopian. It is true now, as it was not true before the nineteenth century, that under modern conditions of scientific, totalitarian, national warfare civilization and war are incompatible. You may have the one or you may have the other, but you cannot have both. This is itself a " reality " which even dictators and all those who maintain that war is a reality and permanent peace utopian will have to face. For over twenty-five years now many socialists, democrats, and pacifists have maintained that the conditions of war have changed in such a way that Europeans will have either to abolish it or to abolish their civilization. The events of the last twenty-five years and the present situation of European nations prove that this statement is literally true. The reasons for this are two. The first is the devastation and destruction caused by modern armaments. If Europe is to be subjected at intervals of twenty-five years to the experience of 1914 to 1918—only more so—or if many countries are periodically to be subjected to the recent experiences of Spain and Poland, the surviving inhabitants will, no doubt, survive, but to call their life civilized would be an anachronism.

The second reason is less obvious, but, if anything, more important. The scale of modern totalitarian warfare is so vast and the penalty of unpreparedness so overwhelming that the probability, even the possibility, of war makes a civilized life impossible. The ten years which preceded the outbreak of the war of 1939 showed that war is now a whole-time job for the whole nation even when it is at peace. During that time the German nation was at peace, but it was living under conditions which at any other time in the world's history would have been called war conditions. It is clear that if, when this war is over, we continue to live under the threat of yet another war, all the inhabitants of territory owned by Great Powers or of territory adjoining Great Powers will have to adjust themselves to living permanently as the German people lived from 1931 to 1938—only more so. There used to be something called "the iron law of wages" which was popular in the nineteenth century as an argument for keeping the workers in their places. It was imaginary. But there is nothing imaginary in the iron law of the economics of totalitarian warfare. The economics of modern war will force every nation to sacrifice everything, as Germany has sacrificed everything, to being "prepared" and economically self-sufficient. It must be ready at a moment's notice to pass smoothly from the conditions of armed peace to those of war, and for safety's sake there must be very little difference between them. The nation will therefore have to live permanently on a war footing, its citizens ticketed, docketed, regimented, and trained for war. The standard of living will become appropriate for

36

a community in which private and public wealth
is devoted to the exacting task of paying for the
last war and preparing for the next. The air-raid
shelters and the sirens will always have to be ready
and so will the vast army of citizens belonging to
three-lettered organizations. Presumably in the
intervals between wars the school-children will
return to their homes, the lights will go up in our
streets, and the curtains will come down from our
windows ; the blackout of lighted cities and houses
will be suspended. But the black-out of civilized
life will be permanent, both in peace and in war.

I have tried in the previous pages to give a rather
summary analysis of the real nature of war, its
relation to national policy, and the effect of its
modern development upon human society in
Europe. Whether it has some peculiar " reality "
which makes it inevitable, and therefore all conscious and deliberate efforts and plans to eliminate
it " utopian ", will be discussed later. Before that
discussion is embarked upon, it will be well to
examine briefly our present position, so far as it
affects the problem of international organization
and war and peace, and the events which have
brought us into that position. I propose rather
illogically to begin in the middle. The middle is
the war of 1914–1918, and it is the middle because
no one can understand the war of 1939 who does
not understand the causes of the war of 1914.

The war of 1914 lasted for four years ; it was the

first large-scale, modern totalitarian war. Practically all the states of Europe were involved and they
were divided into two groups or alliances. It was
a test of power as between these two groups. During
the four years the whole of Europe was subjected to
the rule of force and violence, for one half of its
inhabitants were attempting to impose its will upon
the other half by force or violence. What exactly
the will of either side was in 1914 and in 1918 is
not easy to describe accurately or shortly. The
will was often defined by the combatants themselves
in the form of " war aims " or " peace aims ", just
as to-day the statesmen of Germany, France, and
Britain from time to time inform the world and
themselves what they are fighting for. The war
aims of the national leaders of 1914 and 1918 are
usually now simply dismissed with contempt as
lying propaganda or with derision because of the
sequel. To treat them thus is a profound mistake.
If war is an inevitable reality because it is a test of
national power and the instrument of national
policy, then surely it is of the utmost importance to
know what was the object of national policy for
which a war was fought and what the effect of
winning or losing the war was upon that object.
The leaders of the allies repeatedly stated that one
object of their national policy for which they were
fighting the war was to make the world safe for
democracy. They won the war and imposed their
will upon Germany in 1918. In 1928 it was

obvious that the world was far less safe for democracy than it was in 1908.  That is a relevant fact which requires serious investigation.  You have not settled the matter by ridiculing President Wilson as a " professor ", by proclaiming the failure of democracy, and by adjuring us all to get on with the task of fighting the next war.  The fact remains that millions of people thought that they were fighting to make the world safe for democracy and that, after winning that war, they now find that they are doing the same thing all over again.  If national policy means anything at all, it is a fact that the last war was fought for the national policy of making the world safe for democracy.  If it was won and the world became unsafe for democracy, the question arises whether winning a war or, in other words, making the national power effective and enforcing the national will against others is after all a successful method of protecting democracy.

Another object of national policy for which the war was fought was undoubtedly connected with the independence and liberty of small nations, and this war aim became crystallized by the end of the war in the popular slogan of the " right of self-determination ".  The war actually began with an attack by Austria, supported by Germany, upon Serbia.  The Austrian government certainly had legitimate grievances against the Serbian government, but their demands and the final rejection of the Serbian offer went far beyond them.  The Austro-German handling of Serbia was an admirable example of a typical transaction in pure power politics, with the threat of force in the background and ending with the threat translated into actuality, namely war. The Austro-German claims were based entirely upon power ; they implied that the relation between the interests of a large or more powerful state and those of a small or less powerful state was a question to be decided solely by the government of the large, powerful state. This meant that the relations themselves should and would be determined by power, and by power alone ; the large state would dictate its will to the obedient small state, because, if the small state said no, it would be " destroyed " by war. If this claim were admitted, there would be no independence or liberty for small national states in Europe ; for they would either be dictated to by the Great Powers or their populations would be forcefully incorporated in those of the large, power-ful nations. The existence of the small national state and the " right of self-determination " are the negation of pure power politics. There can be no doubt that the statesmen of the allied nations thought—many of them genuinely—that one of their most important war aims was the independence of small nations and the right of self-determination.

The allied statesmen won the war and made the peace. Much can be said—and has been said by the present writer among many others—against the peace of 1918. As between the allies and Germany,

it was largely based upon power ; in history and
international relations those who take to the sword
sooner or later perish by the sword. *Vae victis*, woe
to the conquered, is the very heart and meaning of
power politics, and it is not for those who worship
this idol, power, and never see its cold and clay
feet, to complain when their false god betrays them
and they hear him hiss in their own ear : *Vae victis*.
The conquered suffered in the defeat of 1918 and,
from the liberal and democratic point of view, the
peace imposed—the word itself shows its significant
connection with power—was unjust and dishonest.
But in the main, in other directions, it was a genuine
attempt to translate the war aims into realities.
This was certainly the case with regard to the
liberty and independence of the small state and to
the right of self-determination. These principles
were applied on a large and drastic scale everywhere in Europe, except in the few, but highly
important cases, when they were over-ridden by
the conflicting principle of *vae victis*. If international
relations in Europe were to be determined, not
simply by power and force, but by the right of
national groups to remain or become the citizens
of small states and by the right of small states to
liberty and " justice ",[1] then the Europe of 1919

[1] The word justice is used in many senses ; one of its meanings
implies that as between the conflicting interests of the strong and
the weak, power and force should not be the sole determinant of
which interests are to prevail. That is the sense in which the
word is used above.

was a better, a freer, and a juster continent than the Europe of 1913. Now look round upon the Europe of 1940. It is at war again and it appears to be fighting the same war for the same objects which the allied statesmen thought that they were fighting for from 1914 to 1918—and they not only thought they were fighting for them, they were fighting for them, and, when they won, they to a large extent translated those aims into realities.

To all simple-minded persons, among whom the present writer includes himself, this must be a puzzling and disquieting fact ; to those who regard power as the ultimate political reality it ought to be even more disquieting, if they are on the British front of the battle line. During the last few years or months we have seen certain things happen in Austria, in Czechoslovakia, in Poland, and in Finland. These events have all been connected with the birth or death of nations or states. Violent death has approached four European states ; in three cases the powerful German state has extinguished the life, destroyed the liberty and independence, of three smaller states, Austria, Czechoslovakia, and Poland, and, as I write, the Russian Soviet Government is attempting to do the same thing to the small state of Finland. These small states which are dead or are dying were all born with the peace treaties of 1918. We fought the last war in order that they might be born and we are fighting the present war apparently, because they are dead or in order that they may be resurrected.

If these facts mean what they appear to mean, we fought the last war in order to establish an international society in which the small state should have an assured right to existence, *lebensraum*, and liberty and independence—in other words a Europe in which the interests of the smaller and less powerful states should not be determined by the will of the great and powerful states. That was our national policy. Our policy was challenged by Germany and Austria, which denied the right of Serbians, Czechs, and Poles to exist as independent communities in separate states. The question was put to the test of war or of power. It was settled by power in favour of our national policy and against that of Germany. Austria, Yugoslavia, Czechoslovakia, Poland were born from the war as children of our national policy, the sovereign independent states of the new Europe. Twenty years later the new Europe, Austria, Czechoslovakia, and Poland have disappeared, and we are fighting the same war with the same national policy against the same enemy all over again.

The fact suggests several questions. The first should be put to those who maintain that power must always be a primary and determining reality in the relations between states. If that be the case, it is obviously, as things go, an extremely inefficient and unsatisfactory determinant for the unhappy

Europeans who are thus forced helplessly to suffer its determination in the twentieth century. I cannot believe that even the most realist statesman or political theorist will regard as satisfactory an international system which requires that the right of the Czechs to an independent state has to be vindicated by power at the cost of four years of European war in 1918 and then has to be vindicated again at the same cost and by the same method in 1938. Moreover this again suggests a further awkward question for the power school of statesmen and thinkers. If they are right in regarding power as the determining factor in international society, are they not in supporting the national policy of the wars of 1914 and 1939 pursuing two contradictory objects? Germany is, and for the next 100 years will probably remain, however often defeated, a more powerful state than Czechoslovakia. If power is the determining factor in the relations between states, the superior power of Germany will always determine Germany's relations to Czechoslovakia, and if it is the will of the German government that Czechoslovakia shall not exist, Czechoslovakia will not exist. You may force Germany by a temporary coalition of powerful states and by defeat in war to recognize the temporary existence of Czechoslovakia, but if power reigns supreme, unless you somehow or other contrive to make Germany permanently less powerful than Czechoslovakia, the existence or non-existence of the weaker state will be

44

determined by the will or national policy of the stronger.

I do not myself believe—and I shall later give reasons for this—that there is some peculiar " reality " in power as a factor in human, and particularly international, society, and that it therefore must necessarily be a primary determinant in human and international relations. On the contrary, it is an extremely unstable and elusive factor, largely dependent for its social effect upon men's ideas and the way in which they themselves determine to order their way of life. The power of a physically strong man over a physically weak man as a determinant of their relations depends upon how they themselves regard that power and how they themselves choose to order the society in which they live. If I go into the town of Lewes this afternoon, I shall knock up against hundreds of people, some of whom I know and others of whom are strangers. All kinds of social questions may arise between us, of buying and selling, legal rights and obligations, courtesy and discourtesy. Whatever happens to us this afternoon, whatever difficulties, disputes, or conflict of interests may arise between us, it will never cross the mind of a single one of us that we differ in physical strength and therefore in power ; we have simply dismissed from our mind the possibility of that very " real " factor, that particular variety of power, having any relevance to or effect upon our social relations. And therefore it has no relevance and no effect. The power is quite " real ", but as a factor determining social relations it no longer exists. But if I had made the same four-miles journey into Lewes five or six centuries ago, I and everyone whom I met on the road and in the streets would have had this factor constantly in mind as highly relevant to our relations. And it was relevant because people's attitude towards that kind of power was in those days different from ours and they ordered their society in such a way that it was an important factor. *A priori* there seems to be no reason to believe that power has a different nature and reality in international society from what it has in national society or that it is not equally amenable to elimination and control in both. To those who take this view the argument in the preceding paragraph does not apply, for their answer will probably be that it is precisely because we have tried to make power the supreme reality and determining factor in the relations between states that we have landed ourselves in the present impasse.

Nevertheless, even those who take my view, who deny any peculiar reality to power, and who believe that there is no reason why it should eternally have a dominating place in international relations, must regard the facts behind the argument with disquietude. For many of us hold that it was right for the Empire to fight with France and Belgium against Germany in 1914, and still more of us hold that it was right to resist the aggressions of the Nazi government even at the risk of war in 1938 and 1939. The fact that we won the war of 1914 and that the winning of it seems to have done no good at all, for we are now fighting it all over again, is almost as awkward for us as it is for the realists and power politicians. For inevitably, if we do not ask the question of ourselves, it will be put to us by other people : If you fought the war of 1914 against Germany for democracy, the right of self-determination, and the liberty of small nations, won it, and yet found it impossible to protect democracy, self-determination, and small states, is there any conceivable reason why you should succeed by war in 1939 when you failed in 1914 ?

The whole of this book will, I hope, show the answer which I personally would make to this question, but it stares one so menacingly in the face at this point that, in order to prevent misunderstanding, I propose to anticipate the argument and give summarily the answer as I see it. It is true that, if British war aims in 1914 were peace, democracy, liberty, and the rights of small nations, the war was won but was unsuccessful. It is true that we seem to be fighting it all over again for the same objects. I see no certainty, no probability even, that, if we win this war, we shall be any more successful in achieving our objects than we were in 1918. Yet I believe that we were right to resist the Nazi policy of aggression against the small states of Europe even at the risk of war, and therefore that we were right, when that government accepted the challenge, to go to war.

There is no quibble or refusal to face " facts " in this position.  In politics and society, just as in one's ordinary life, when a decision to act has to be made, all that is open for one is often only a choice between evils.  To-morrow in the middle of the night I may wake up to find that my house is on fire.  I open the door of the bedroom and see the flames already roaring in the passage and cutting me off from the staircase.  I open the window and see a drop of 30 feet into the garden.  What am I to do ?  Wait in the room on the chance that a fire-escape will reach me before I am suffocated by the smoke and then roasted alive, or jump into the garden and run the risk of breaking my legs or my neck ?  It is not my choice or my fault that my house is in flames ;  the cause of the conflagration dates from months or years back, a faulty flue or a faulty electrical installation.  Now events and facts force a choice upon me, and a choice between two evils.  I shall not evade the issue by getting into bed again, pulling the bedclothes over my head, and cursing the plumbers and the electricians.  And when I look out of my window or through the window of *The Times* newspaper at the Europe of 1939 and 1940, I feel that I am in much the same situation and faced with the same kind of choice.  This vast, ramshackle old house which we call Europe is on fire, and we are all faced with the ugly choice of staying where we are with the probability of being later burnt alive or of jumping out of the window with the probability of breaking our necks. Are we to wait, to allow the governments of Germany and Italy (and now Russia) to pursue unresisted their policy of aggression against small states, gradually destroying their independence, and making the rule of power and force the only rule of law for Europe? Are we to wait, arming and rearming, living in a state of perpetual " preparedness " and a perpetual crisis, on the chance that when the dictators have devoured the small fry they will be content and leave the large, fat carp alone? Or are we to say that we stand for a system of law, order, liberty, and peace in Europe and that if that system is deliberately and systematically attacked, we will resist the aggressor and the aggression? Are we to act on this, on the chance that the system of violence and aggression may be stayed by force and that then the system of law, order, liberty and peace may be more firmly re-established?

The choice is a nasty choice between two immense evils. But you cannot escape it by pretending that it is something different. You cannot escape it by drawing the bedclothes of pacifism, communism, isolationism or some other -ism over your head, cursing the politicians, and saying that it is not your fault or your concern if the house is on fire— you will be burnt alive just the same and, as the

49

smoke of your burning body rises to heaven, the cynical gods will not applaud the sacrifice. The choice is there, dictated by the situation, events, and facts. It is a choice of evils in which a reasonable decision can only be made by a cool calculation of probabilities.

It is not surprising that many reasonable and intelligent people choose the first alternative. They think that the last war showed that the chance of establishing liberty, justice, law, order and peace in international society after a great war is negligible, and that therefore we should have done better to " keep out of it " and to keep out of Europe, trusting that something would turn up to make the tide recede or the wheels begin revolving in the opposite direction, for instance a war in the East, a change of heart in Hitler, or even his conviction that the British Empire is too strong or too good to be attacked by Germany. People who take this view and make this choice have strong arguments and facts on their side. Nevertheless, I think they are wrong. In the Europe of 1930 to 1940 the relations of states were largely determined by power and force. The British government, no less than the governments of Hitler and Mussolini, accepted that system. There is where the trouble lies, for the Nazi policy of aggression is the logical result of that system, its *reductio ad absurdum* by fanatics. Even at the height of the appeasement policy, Mr. Chamberlain and the National Government made no attempt to contract out of the system of force and violence (and even if they had attempted it, they could not have done so) ; they came forward with appeasement in one hand and rearmament in the other. They said in effect : " We are not going to resist aggression against Czechoslovakia, but we will resist aggression against Belgium, France, or the Seychelles Islands "—and in the end they resisted aggression against Poland.

That is what made this policy of " keeping out of it " to all intents and purposes impossible. The only possibility of keeping out of it was by a policy of complete pacifism and disarmament—I do not think it would have been or would be successful, and in any case no British government would adopt it or remain in office twenty-four hours if it did so. The worst of all attitudes in a world of lawless violence, where power and the gangster rule—the world of Europe to-day—is to go about heavily armed and to assure the highwaymen, the gangsters, and the starving poor that you will under no circumstances use your weapons—and Mr. Chamberlain's policy of appeasement at one moment came perilously near to that. It is at any rate a conceivable procedure to go about unarmed and trust to God ; but if you carry a pistol, even if you still trust in God, it is imperative to keep your powder dry and to make it clear that, if attacked, you will trust in God and shoot.

Under those circumstances, if you are prepared

and determined to shoot in case you are attacked,
and if at the same time your object is to abolish the
pistols and to establish a society based upon law,
order, and liberty instead of upon pistols and
shooting, the real question is not whether to resist,
but when and in what circumstances to resist.
Here is the choice of evils ; you cannot escape it.
You have or will have to resist because you are
part of a system, part of a society based upon power,
force, aggression, and resistance. If you wish to
change the system, it is probable that you may have
a better chance of doing so if you make the grounds
and occasion of resistance not an attack upon yourself, but aggression against others and the system
itself. For by that policy you will get allies to help
you to resist the aggressor and even possibly to
change the whole system, if your resistance is
successful.

One must repeat that, as things are to-day, even
if the Nazi government is beaten, the chances of
changing the system after a successful war are not
very great. To change the system requires a certain
amount of reason, intelligence, and common sense
in the inhabitants of Europe, and the inhabitants
of Europe are to-day not rational, intelligent, or
sensible. All that one can say is that, if Hitler is
defeated and the Nazi government disappears from
Germany, there is just an outside chance that there
will be a sufficient number of Europeans with a
sufficient amount of intelligence and common sense,

52

provoked by the miseries of two wars in twenty years, to take the necessary steps to change their international system of power politics and war. On the other hand, if Hitler were not resisted and he were allowed to pursue his path of conquest over the small states of Europe, a vast area would be subjected to the most gruesome regime of violence, tyranny, and cruelty and in the end we should find ourselves fighting just the same, but with far less chance of success.

This is a digression from my argument, but it is a relevant digression. For it reveals the roots of the problem of war and peace in modern Europe. The roots are to be found in power and force, national and international, and the place which power and force are given in the relations of states —and " the relations of states " mean in fact (though people rarely remember it) the actual lives of all the inhabitants of Europe who are the citizens of those states. Whether we have war or whether we have peace depends not upon the inevitability of war, the utopianism of peace, or the " reality " of power, but upon the place which we assign to national power and force in our lives and in the lives of all other good or bad Europeans. It was not the Kaiser who made the war of 1914, but the system of power politics of which he was, with his mailed fist and German sword, the flamboyant, rather ridiculous, and wholly disastrous figurehead. It is not even Hitler who made the war of 1939,

a pitiable emigrant from the mental underworld of
neurotic fear, envy, and sadism, but the system of
power and force of which he is the disastrous
*reductio ad absurdum.*

Let us return to the point from which we started
on the digression. The war of 1914, we had seen,
was a test of national power ; it was a struggle
between two groups of states to impose their national
policies by force upon each other. Our group won
and we proceeded, not apparently with much
success, to impose our policy upon the other. The
war had lasted for four years and it had had a
profound effect, not only upon states, governments,
and frontiers, but upon the minds and bodies of
millions of ordinary individuals who survived it.
This is a fact in the determination of history which
statesmen and historians, now that the fact has
itself become history, are apt to neglect or forget.
It is, however, a fact which must be remembered
and investigated.

A world war or a European war of any magnitude
allows the ordinary man, as well as the political
theorist, to see and indeed to feel the reality of
power and force when they are allowed to dominate
and determine nakedly international society and
therefore our lives. For four years, from 1914 to
1918, power and force were allowed to play this
rôle in Europe. All our lives were ordered on a
system in which we were all trying to make the lives
of other people so unbearable that they would do

what we wanted them to do, and therefore, by the
iron law of power, force, and human misery, we
were all engaged upon the laborious task of killing
one another in large numbers. The human race
is—as you may learn by listening to broadcasters
and the realist school of political writers—neither
rational nor intelligent, but it has sufficient reason
and intelligence to be able to kill itself in large
numbers and make its own life unbearable on a
colossal scale, if it gives its mind to it. It is, owing
to the laws of psychology, politics, and economics,
as we are so often told, unable to make peace or
its own communal life tolerably happy, but it is
quite capable of making war and its own life a hell.
It did so with the greatest success from August,
1914, to November, 1918.

The strange thing is that people, the ordinary
people, the individuals who live in London or in
Sussex, in Berlin or the plains of Prussia, in Paris
or in the valley of the Dordogne, these people everywhere did not like it. In all these places, all over
Europe they were saying in their different tongues
the same two words : " Never again." That was
itself a political reality of some importance and the
statesmen and rulers therefore had to pay attention
to it, to listen respectfully, at any rate for a moment,
to what the millions of ordinary people were saying.
What they were saying was that in their humble
opinion war was no longer a tolerable method of
settling affairs in modern Europe, that it made life

unbearable even for those whom it did not kill, that the statesmen and rulers must find some other method of doing their business, for in future the common people would refuse to be either heroes or cannon-fodder—" never again ". If enough people at the same time say the same thing and mean it, even the Great King, the absolute monarch, and the dictator, not to speak of the democratic Prime Minister or President, have to pay attention to it —which shows that psychology, no less than power, is a political reality which may determine history.

In 1919 there were in Europe a good many kings, quite a few Presidents, any number of Prime Ministers and statesmen who had won or lost the Great War. Taken together they may not unfairly be called the ruling classes. They heard these words, " never again ", echoing up and down Europe, rumbling and grumbling among soldiers clamouring to be demobilized, among munition workers waiting to be unemployed, and among agricultural labourers waiting for the houses which should be fit for heroes to live in. The ruling classes knew that the promises of the war were about to come home to roost upon their innocent heads, that there was a nasty time before them, and that, when so many people were saying " never again ", something must be done about it. What they did was to establish the League of Nations.

In high places the spokesman of the common people of the world in 1919 was an American,

# War

Woodrow Wilson, President of the United States of America. It has become customary, in view of what has happened since, to sneer at President Wilson as a professor, an intellectual and liberal, an unpractical doctrinaire, a dreamer from utopia whom realists like M. Clemenceau and Mr. Lloyd George put in his place, though unfortunately they had to insert one of his liberal fantasies, the Covenant, in the realities of the Versailles treaty.[1] If this be so, it is a strange thing that during the last years of the war and the first years of peace the common people all over the world were convinced that the one statesman who was interpreting their thoughts and speaking their language was the President. We are usually told that the people, otherwise called the mob, rightly refuse to look for their leaders and interpreters among intellectuals, doctrinaires, and theorists. One would hardly expect a politician who confined himself to the intellectual " exposition of fundamentals " to become a great popular leader among men who had spent four years in the trenches. If so, the fact that the extremely practical experience of four years in the trenches should bring ordinary men, untutored and uncorrupted by the use of

[1] E.g. *The Twenty Years' Crisis, 1919–1939*, by Professor E. H. Carr, p. 20 : " . . . utopianism with its insistence on general principles may be said to represent the characteristic intellectual approach to politics. Woodrow Wilson, the most perfect modern example of the intellectual in politics, ' excelled in the exposition of funda-mentals. . . . His political method . . . was to base his appeal upon broad and simple principles, avoiding commitment upon specific measures '."

reason or of their intellect, to the unusual conviction that the exposition of political fundamentals by an American professor, who was so misguided as to use his reason and intellect, exactly interpreted the result of their experience is itself of considerable significance. It is a political phenomenon which even the most realist professor, like Professor Carr, should meditate on, for it might throw a new light for him upon the nature of political utopias and political realities.

After all, what the ordinary man had discovered (shall we say, by his experience ?) and President Wilson (shall we say, by his reason ?) was simply that war is an intolerable thing. To say that war is an intolerable thing is of course to expound a fundamental and to state a broad and simple principle. It is worth while remembering that at the end of the previous great European war, the war that was fought up and down Europe by Napoleon's armies for nearly twenty years at the beginning of the nineteenth century, ordinary men and women, at any rate in Britain, became obsessed by a fundamental or general principle of much the same kind ; whereas in 1918 they had become convinced that war is intolerable, in 1815 they became convinced that slavery is intolerable, and by making this discovery they also found themselves in agreement with the broad and simple principle about slavery which had been enunciated by many utopian intellectuals. Who knows ? May it per-

haps be that Professor Carr and the practical statesmen have overlooked the fact that some broad and
simple principles contain important political truths ?
That after a great war the miseries of ordinary
persons may have jogged them into thinking and
into discovering for themselves—by experience—
that certain things, like slavery and war, *are* intolerable in modern society ?  May it not even be true
that slavery and war, like cannibalism, head-
hunting, or witch-burning, are intolerable in the
Europe of 1800 or 1900 ?

The common people of 1815 had, at any rate,
decided that slavery was an intolerable thing.  If
a thing is socially intolerable, the only thing to do
is to abolish it and that is what the people demanded
of their statesmen and ruling classes.  Their demand
was so insistent that, although many practical men
and professors proved that it was utopian to attempt
to abolish slavery, it was in the face of considerable
opposition and with some difficulty abolished.  The
beginning of the process was in 1918 much the same
as it had been in 1815.  The common people said :
" War is an intolerable thing—never again " ;  the
practical men and the realist professors said : " Power
is a reality ;  force is a reality ;  war is inevitable ;
peace is utopian " ;  but the voice of the common
people was so insistent that the statesmen at Versailles thought that they would have to do something
about it—they must abolish war, or at least appear
to take some important steps towards abolishing war.

59

What they did was to establish the League of Nations. It is important to understand why they did this, what the League was intended to do, and what in fact it was. It is true that the establishment of the League was due to reasoning. If you read Professor Carr's book to which reference has just been made or any other of the many attacks, now going about, upon the League, President Wilson, liberalism, internationalism, or democracy, you would imagine that the fact that the construction of a League of Nations was the end of a process of ratiocination, was absolutely damning to it and ensured its failure. You would infer from this kind of criticism that only the utopian theorist in politics ever uses his reason or decides what should be done in order to obtain a desired result by arguing from a broad and simple principle and applying it in accordance with experience to a particular set of circumstances ; on the contrary, if you took these critics according to their word, you would conclude that the only practical and successful statesmen are those who never use their reason and have never heard of a " fundamental ", a general principle, or even a general statement.[1] This view of politics, statesmanship, and history is, if one may for once

---

[1] It is only fair to Professor Carr to say that he contradicts in the latter part of his book almost everything which he says in the first part, but that is because in the second half he attempts to tell us what ought to be done about it, i.e. to prevent war, and he is then, of course, forced to proceed exactly in the same way as the " utopians " proceeded in their attempt to find a way of preventing war.

use plain language, just nonsense. Every one uses their reason, " fundamentals ", and broad and simple principles in making political decisions or judgments, or indeed in making any practical decision or judgment, and in ninety-nine cases out of a hundred they use them in the same way. They differ, not in either working or not working from principles to particular cases through experience, but in the kind of principles they hold, the rightness or wrongness of their reasoning, and the way in which they allow their emotions and desires to affect their reasoning, their judgment, and their principles. This remains true even though it is notorious that it is a common thing for everyone, whether realist or utopian statesmen, dictators or professors, intellectuals or agricultural labourers, first to decide to do what they want to do and then find the reasons and principles which show that they were quite right to do it. This only means that we all are inclined to allow our emotions and desires to determine both our principles and our judgments—and if you look round the world to-day, we do so, I suggest, with the most disastrous results both to ourselves and to everyone else.

Let us examine one or two examples of this process. X is a professional burglar and Y, his next-door neighbour, is a respectable, law-abiding citizen either working eight hours a day for a wage of between 35*s*. and 45*s*. or " on the dole ". It is probable that neither of them has ever stated con-

sciously to himself as " fundamentals " or broad and
simple principles the motives or reasons which have
led one of them to choose burglary and the other
wage-slavery as the better method of earning a
living.   But it would be quite possible and profitable
to do this accurately for them ; it is psychologically
true that their actions are determined by these
different broad and simple principles and it remains
true even though, as is certainly the case, those
principles have been determined by their individual
instincts or desires.   It is also possible profitably to
examine in the light of actual experience the effects
upon society and upon the individual of the two
principles when translated into practice, and to
decide, in the light of that investigation, which is
" better ", i.e. which has in fact the more desirable
results—for society and for the individual—the
principle that honest wage-slavery is a better method
of earning a living than robbery with violence or
the principle which says vice versa.   It is fashionable
to-day to maintain that in this process which involves
the formulation (unconsciously) of general principles and which is concerned with ends rather than
means reason plays no part at all, that our action is
determined purely instinctively, appetitively, or
emotionally, that, as we are so often told, we first
want something or want to do something and then
discover the reasons why it is a good thing or why
it is good that we should do it.   I believe this
picture to be an over-simplification which is a

travesty of human psychology, as anyone may discover by watching carefully the working of his own mind or that of his neighbours. Everyone of course often acts instinctively and everyone is continually rationalizing his desires, but it is not true that the ends or objects of our actions, particularly in our relations with other human beings, are determined solely by our instincts, desires, and emotions. They are determined by a complicated process in which reason, instincts, desires, and emotions interact. It is false psychology and misleading political psychology to ignore the interaction and to pretend that reason never affects and inhibits the desires. It often does so and therefore, when it does, it plays a great part in determining our aims and objects and " principles ".

Let us return to the burglar. The burglar acts on the " fundamental " or broad and simple principle that burglary is a better way of earning a living than digging dirt or going on the dole. I do not say that he consciously states this generalization to himself or that he has reached it rationally ; he " accepts " it in a vague, semi-conscious way and—what is perhaps more important—it affects his actions. And though it is not true that he has reached this vague, semi-conscious principle by the use of reason, it is equally untrue to say that reason has not influenced him at all in arriving at it ; instinct, desires, and reasoning applied to his own and other people's experience have produced the

final mental state which determines him to be pro-
fessionally a burglar and not a navvy.  But there
is another way in which reasoning plays its part in
the mind and actions of burglars.  His instincts,
desires, and principles have created his object—to
burgle houses as the means to a living ; he now has
to " attain his object " by the burgling of a particular house.  Even the burglar then has to consider the best way in which to burgle houses and a
particular house.  If he attempts to do this solely
by instinct, desire, and emotion, or even—may one
add—by conditioned reflexes, he will not be a very
successful burglar.  He attains his object, he decides
what is the best way to burgle houses and which is
the best house to burgle, by applying reason to his
experience, and his success as a burglar will depend
to a considerable extent upon the way in which he
uses his reason and his experience.

In all these respects the art of statesmanship is
just like the art of burglary, as indeed is the art of
doing anything which requires a protracted and
organized effort to attain a somewhat complex
object.  Take Bismarck, for instance.  Bismarck is
usually represented by the realist and power
politicians to have been the most realist of all
nineteenth-century statesmen, the precise opposite
of a man like President Wilson.  Yet Bismarck's
statesmanship and policy was founded on methods
and mental procedure no different from those of the
burglar.  Before 1870 he started with a funda-

mental, a broad and general principle, that the unification of Germany was desirable. Many people had before tried without success to unify Germany and there were theorists and statesmen between 1830 and 1870 who argued that such unification was utopian, that the nature of Germans and of German politics made it impossible. Bismarck arrived at this broad principle, at his political object, partly emotionally, because he was a man of a certain kind of character, and partly by reason. I do not think that anyone who reads his life and his sayings can doubt this ; they show that he desired the unification of Germany partly instinctively as an end in itself, and partly as a means to other things, e.g. to power. But the process by which he arrived at the conclusion that the unification of Germany was desirable as a means, i.e. to power, was determined by reasoning, in fact by arguing from fundamentals to particulars. Having determined his political principles and his primary political object, Bismarck then proceeded to work out the best way of actually attaining his object. From 1860 to 1870 by applying reason to experience he elaborated an extraordinarily complicated and subtle series of strategems, punctuated by outbursts of force or war, with this object in view. He succeeded. But no statesman has ever formulated more clearly to himself his political fundamentals or has worked out more " intellectually " the means for attaining them than this realist—and that per-

haps explains his success.   Indeed, he treated foreign
policy rather like a series of mathematical problems
which could be solved by the use of right principles,
formulæ, and the manipulation of men and armies.
His reinsurance treaty with Russia is a good example
of this method and his dread of " imponderables ",
as he called them, i.e. events which you could not
foresee or factors hidden from your view, is directly
related to it, for it implied that, if only you knew
all the factors in a political situation, you could work
it out like a chess problem.

I must apologize once more for dealing at such great
length with these kinds of truisms and unimportant
facts like the mental processes of burglars, unemployed navvies, and great statesmen.   Nearly all
politicians and writers who tell you that war is (or
is not) inevitable, that peace or the League of
Nations is (or is not) utopian, ignore them, giving
you instead sweeping statements about the " reality "
of power, the possibility of this or the impossibility
of that, about practical men and doctrinaire professors.   Eighty per cent. of these general statements
are irrelevant to the understanding of history and
the solution of political problems.   If you want to
know whether it is possible to prevent war and, if it
is, what is the best way to set about it, you must
first know what goes on in the minds of burglars,
statesmen, and other people when they pursue aims
or objects involving relations with individuals or
groups of individuals, and secondly what factors in

a particular case make successful achievement of the
aim possible, probable, improbable, or impossible.

The point had been reached in our argument in
which it had become apparent that the mental
processes of Bismarck, when formulating a national
policy and pursuing it, were in their nature no
different from those of a burglar, when pursuing his
object of making a living by breaking into houses.
The mental processes of President Wilson and those
who helped to establish the League of Nations in
order to prevent war were no different from those
of the burglars and of Bismarck. They did not
differ from them by formulating " fundamentals "
or broad and simple principles and then attempting
to translate the principle into practice or the object
or " ideal " into success by applying reason to
experience. This becomes clear if you examine the
way in which the League idea came into existence
and was then translated into practice. President
Wilson and others who put forward the idea started
with a fundamental or broad and simple principle,
namely that it was desirable to prevent war, because
war in modern society is intolerable. This " principle " that the prevention of war is desirable is
exactly the same kind of " principle " as that from
which Bismarck started, namely that the unification
of Germany was desirable. The one is no more
intellectual or theoretical or prima facie utopian
than the other ; each is or was an object or aim of
policy, or an ideal, if you like to call it so.

## The War for Peace

The principle or ideal of preventing war set a political problem to those who held it. They treated the problem of how to prevent war exactly as Bismarck treated the problem of how to unify Germany. Bismarck turned to history and experience in order first to discover what the factors were in 1850 to 1860 which were primarily responsible for preventing the union of the various German states and principalities, and then by applying reason to experience he devised methods of great cunning and complexity in order to eliminate the factors producing disunity and to promote unity. His treatment of Austria, for instance, culminating in the war of 1866, was directed to eliminate Austria, which he considered an element promoting disunity, from the German confederation ; his treatment of France, culminating in the war of 1870, was directed to drawing the other German states together in a common national purpose under the leadership of Prussia. He argued rightly from the experience of history that, once Austria had been eliminated, nothing was more likely to effect a permanent union of " Germany " under a Prussian hegemony, than common action in such a war.

Those who aimed at preventing war in the twentieth century treated their problem just as Bismarck treated his. They began with the examination of the factors which caused war in the twentieth century and they then went on to try to discover means of eliminating them and of encouraging or creating those factors in international society which might promote peaceful co-operation among states. Their first task was necessarily to examine the system which governed the relations of European states before 1914 and out of which arose the war of 1914, in order to see whether it was possible to discover the causes of war in it and then to eliminate them. This is not a doctrinaire, " liberal ", or utopian method of procedure ; it is the procedure which every practical man follows when he wishes to change something which he does not like in his personal, political, or social environment, whether it is water dripping through his ceiling on to his bed, the existence of over a million unemployed, or the danger of bombs being dropped on his head by hostile aeroplanes in periodic wars. No one can examine the history of the nineteenth century and the system by which the relations of European states were governed without seeing certain factors which are clearly connected with the permanent threat and the periodic occurrence of war. It was a system which may be briefly described as based upon power politics. Each state claimed to be sovereign and independent, that is to say its government claimed the absolute power to determine its policy, to judge what was or was not a " vital interest ", and to pursue that interest without any regard for or inter-ference from any other state. In any dispute which might arise between it and the government of another state over any question which it chose to regard as a " vital interest ", it claimed the right to be judge of its own case. Normally, it is true, it admitted that it was bound by such treaties as it or previous governments had signed with the governments of other states and also by the " rules of international law ", but if there were, as there frequently were, disputes over the obligations of treaties or law, it again claimed to be itself the judge and interpreter of its own rights and obligations.

The relations of these states, of the governments, and of the individuals of which they were composed were neither simple nor few. On the contrary, the highly industrialized, mechanized, scientific, capitalist society which developed in the nineteenth century had produced an economic and social life of great complexity continually flowing across and ignoring national or even continental frontiers. Individuals, groups, and governments in the different countries were so closely and so variously bound together in this international economic and social life that the national sovereign independent state as an instrument for regulating their relations was in fact a hopeless anachronism. This was not theory, but in 1914 it was already fact ; the national state, like all anachronisms, did not work ; it had already broken down as an instrument for regulating the relations of governments and people. The signs of its breakdown were that in some directions it had in fact, though not in theory, abandoned its claim to sovereignty and independence, while in others it had in fact, though not perhaps in theory, been superseded by a complicated and wide-spread system of international government.[1]

Behind this network of international relations and of the organization and government which had gradually developed in order to deal with them there remained, however, this anachronistic conception of the sovereign, independent state, the supreme arbiter of its own relations and its own interests. Governments still transacted the affairs of what are called " high politics " [2] according to this ancient and obsolete formula. The interests of states were considered to be normally conflicting, both economically and politically, so that what was a loss to one was a gain to the other.[3] To deal with the relations of these states and governments and these conflicting interests, assumed to be of such overwhelming importance, hardly any organization or machinery of government had been

[1] The growth and character of this international government which developed prior to 1914 are described in my book, *International Government*.

[2] High politics have always been largely concerned with questions and interests, like national honour, prestige, and the possession of bits of territory, which have no importance or value, and often no meaning, for ordinary persons or 99·999 per cent. of the citizens of the states who quarrelled over them. They have nevertheless been the object or causes of war.

[3] The belief that the interests of states are normally conflicting is a pure delusion or assumption, yet we are frequently told that it is one of the stern realities of international politics. It would be just as sensible to assume that the interests of people living in different streets or different towns, or that the interests of people with grey eyes and blue eyes normally are conflicting. The point will be considered more fully below.

suffered to grow. A parish council in a small village had more equipment for dealing intelligently and practically with the affairs of a few dozen houses and families than had statesmen for dealing with those of Europe or the world. There were no regular or rational methods of making the rules, regulations, or laws which were necessary for any peaceful and efficient control of the relations between states and the vast populations of Europe. In general, the only way of arriving at an agreement on such matters was by means of treaties, laboriously negotiated between the governments of individual states, and even the validity of such agreements was always in doubt, because it was always doubtful whether the sovereign independent state might not at any moment claim the right to denounce a treaty or repudiate an obligation. There was no regular and efficient procedure for settling disputes or difficulties which arose with regard to existing agreements and relations or as the result of a change in circumstances or the growth of new relations. It is true that some states were mutually pledged by treaty to submit certain kinds of disputes to judicial settlement ; but it was almost universally maintained that no state, owing to the sacredness of its sovereignty, could agree to submit to judicial settlement or third party judgment questions which were of real importance to it, i.e. precisely those kinds of questions and disputes which in any society it is most essential to submit to that kind of settlement. In consequence, whenever an important dispute arose and the situation became really dangerous, every state claimed the absolute right to be judge of its own case. Finally, although the nineteenth and twentieth centuries have been an era of tremendous economic, political, and social change all over the world and of one revolution after another in men's psychology, in their beliefs and their desires, there was absolutely no way whatsoever of altering in an orderly and peaceful manner the *status quo*, as it is called, which means simply that it was impossible to alter otherwise than by war the structure of international society in order to adjust it to the needs of a new society and a new man.

Such was the skeleton of the system which Europeans had devised for carrying on the affairs of their closely articulated, extremely complicated, and apparently highly civilized society. If you can imagine Mr. Herbert Morrison trying to administer the affairs of the London County Council in 1940 with the organization and ideas of a tribe of Pacific head-hunting savages, you will have a fairly accurate picture of the Kaiser, the Tsar, Sir Edward Grey, and M. Delcassé managing the affairs of Europe between 1900 and 1914. For the skeleton of human society is moved and worked by the ideas and beliefs of the men who compose it, though the skeleton itself has a reciprocal action and imposes certain limitations upon the ideas. The ideas which were in the heads of these emperors and statesmen and with which they attempted to move the skeleton of European society and order the affairs of Europe were those of what are called power politics. In any society where there is no accepted law and order, no accepted method of resolving differences or of obtaining equitable settlement of disputes, no machinery for changing the *status quo*, no sense of common interests or habit of co-operation, but a continual emotional insistence upon conflicting interests—in such a society what ultimately determines social relations must be power or force. That was why in the years before 1914 governments and statesmen acted on the assumption that the ultimate and most important factor in international politics was power and the organization of national force. The test of power and the final arbiter of policy always therefore lay in the background of all " negotiations "—war. To be prepared for war and to be strong enough to resist or destroy your neighbour and potential enemy was the first duty of statesmanship. Hence the policy of the balance of power, of Mitteleuropa, of the armed truce, of the " two-Power standard ", and of the two great hostile alliances which led in 1914 to war.

This picture of pre-war Europe would not be complete unless we drew attention to certain psychological factors which coloured it. Two are of importance. First, the psychology of large sections of the European ruling classes was still, as was noted above, mediæval. War to them was not merely or even primarily an instrument of national policy—it was the greatest and noblest of all games, an occupation, art, and science proper to kings and aristocrats. The influence of these people upon international politics and the destiny of Europe was by no means negligible, for many of them sat on thrones, were at the head of governments, and commanded armies and navies. The Kaiser, whose mind was like a shuttlecock, is an obvious example, but there were people behind him and behind the policy of most countries who had the same ideas as the Kaiser, who talked less and less ingenuously about them—and were, therefore, the more dangerous.

The psychology of these mediævalists coloured the whole of power politics. It added enormously to the danger of war, but that it was able to exert so great and disastrous an influence upon foreign affairs was due to another psychological fact. Ever since the French Revolution there had developed all over Europe, and in all classes of the population, a highly emotional psychology which we now call nationalism. Its causes and exact nature are complex, but it is unnecessary for our present purpose to analyse or even describe it at any length. In its simplest form it consists of beliefs and desires connected with the group of people to whom one considers oneself bound by the common ties of nationality. Under the influence of the French Revolution it became linked with the ideas of

freedom, government, and the state. All over
Europe people who thought that they belonged to
the same " nationality " developed a passionate
determination to unite under a single government
in a sovereign, independent national state. The
word " passionate " in the previous sentence is
accurate and important. Nationalism was a tre-
mendously emotional ingredient in the social
psychology of the European of the nineteenth
century. And the emotion made it far easier than
it would have otherwise been for the mediævalists
and power politicians to get the ordinary people,
who provide the cannon-fodder, to consent to the
use of totalitarian war as the noblest of games and
the instrument of national power.

Nationalism also increased international anarchy
and the danger of war in another way. The frontiers of few European states have been drawn strictly
on lines of nationality and in many parts of the
continent people of different nationality are so
inextricably mixed together that it is impossible to
draw a frontier without leaving substantial national
minorities in various states. The growth of nationalist sentiment has continually created demands
which could not be satisfied without a redrawing
of state frontiers and often large changes in the
*status quo*. But such changes may and very often
did seriously affect the power of existing states. In
consequence questions of nationalism have for a
hundred years proved the most dangerous and the

most insoluble under a system of power politics and, therefore, the most provocative of war. For they are always highly charged with passion ; they demand a change in the *status quo* and the system itself provides no means of changing the *status quo* without war ; and the change demanded would almost always entail a change in the balance of power itself.

In practice, it is impossible to combine an international system based on self-determination—which is the logical result of nationalism—with an international system based on power and power politics. The two principles are diametrically opposed to each other. For if power and force are to be the ultimate determinants of the relations between states and peoples, how can those relations also be ultimately determined by the right of a small and weak people to govern itself, even if thereby it impairs the " power " of a large state?  The satisfaction of the passion of nationalism and the demand for self-determination throughout Europe are only possible if power politics are abandoned and a system of law and co-operation takes its place.  The attempt to combine the two contradictory systems results naturally in the claim of a Hitler or a Mussolini that the right to self-determination and the claims of nationality are paramount, but only for Germans or Italians, not for Austrians, Czechs, Slovaks, Poles, Finns, Abyssinians, or Albanians. When that stage is reached it is only another step

77

and the right of self-determination has become transformed for the Great Power into the right to *lebensraum*, which for everyone else is the negation of self-determination and nationality, for it means that the power of the powerful state authorizes it to expand and rule at the expense of the weaker. Under such a system nationality and self-determination become the monopoly and privilege of power— the natural result of trying to combine two contradictory systems, self-determination and power politics, for the organization of Europe. And then the last act of the tragedy is inevitable, a clash between two Great Powers, each with its own monopoly and privilege, its own right to *lebensraum*, and its own reliance upon force as the ultimate arbiter of its claims. The last act is a European war.

In the preceding paragraphs I have been describing the European system of inter-state relations as it existed prior to 1914. Those who wished in 1918 to alter the system so as to make war less probable—or at least not inevitable—and the statesmen who thought something must be done to meet the people's demand of " Never again " based their attempt to prevent war upon these facts. They did exactly what Bismarck and the burglar did in similar circumstances. They examined the facts in the light of experience in order to discover, in the light of that experience, which factors were favourable and which were unfavourable to their purpose, and their purpose was to eliminate the unfavourable and to develop and use the favourable factors. Critics of the League and of President Wilson write to-day as if the League was a purely academic, utopian, theoretical construction created out of a political void by the *a priori* reasoning of professors. They speak as if the problem of war and international government was unique and had no relation to experience. Nothing could be further from the truth. To prevent war is a problem of politics and government, not essentially different from the problem of preventing duelling or cock-fighting or of regulating the relations between the inhabitants of Middlesex and those of Surrey. It may be easier to prevent cock-fighting than war or to regulate the relations between Middlesex and Surrey or England and Scotland than those between France and Germany. But there is nothing in the last problem which makes it essentially different from the others. To alter the international system so as to prevent war is simply a problem of human government ; if the object is attainable, it can only be attained, like the objects of Bismarck, by applying reason to experience.

The idea that experience is not available from which we may learn what we shall have to do in Europe if the existing state of affairs is to be altered and wars prevented is ridiculous. It was mentioned above that a Civil Servant in Asia, as an officer of the British Government watching to see

that a murderer was hanged by the neck until he
was dead in accordance with the law, might be
conscious that 3,800 years ago the officers of the
Government of Sumer and Akkad were doing
exactly the same thing not so very far away. That
means that for 4,000 years, at least, human beings
have had experience of communal government.
All that time they have been posing themselves
problems of government, and solving them or failing
to solve them. What are these problems of government ? They are simply questions of how the relations between individuals and groups shall be
ordered and controlled—relations between individual
and individual, between classes, nations, and races,
between groups living in villages, towns, districts, states, or continents. This experience is so
ancient and so catholic that there is nothing which
we cannot learn from it about human government
if we wish to do so. And among the things which
we could most certainly learn from all this experience
is what we must do in the year 1940 if we wish to
prevent another European war. The trouble is not
that the problem is unique or of great complexity
and difficulty, but that we are too stupid and savage
an animal to learn from experience.

The establishment of the League was an attempt
to learn by experience, an attempt to alter the
international inter-state system of the pre-war period
in such a way as to make war less probable or even
to make it improbable. The attempt failed. I shall

later on have to consider at some length the methods
by which it was intended that the League should
perform its functions and the causes of its failure.
Here it is only necessary to draw attention to certain
important facts. It is true that the League was
based upon some broad and simple principles and
that an attempt was made to apply those principles
to Europe and existent states by using reason and
experience. That, as was pointed out above, does
not make the League utopian, theoretical, or
" unreal " and was not the cause of its failure. One
of the principles upon which it was based was that,
if war was to be prevented, the use of force by
national states must be controlled or limited, or to
put it in another way, that the relations of states
must, in some respects, no longer be determined,
as in the past, by their relative power. *A priori*
there is nothing utopian in such a principle applied
to sovereign independent states or in an attempt to
translate it into practice. History is largely a record
of changes in the control and use of power and force
by individuals, classes, and communities in social
relations. The use of power or violence and force
has at certain periods been exercised by the physically strong, by armed civilians, by kings and aristocrats, by employers, by villages, towns, and districts, in order to impose their will upon others or
promote their own interests ; at other periods, the
community has taken steps to prevent the use of
force by the individuals or groups of individuals and

so to control, limit, or eliminate their power as a factor in social relations.

The idea of the League was to control the power of states and to limit the use of force in their relations by methods analogous with those which had proved successful in controlling power and preventing the use of force in the relations of other groups and communities. Some of the causes of its failure may have been in the League itself; those responsible for its creation may have taken the wrong path to the control of national power. That is a question which will have to be carefully considered. But there was one cause of failure external to the League and its system. Societies and historical periods have differed widely from one another in the way in which they organized power and in which force or violence was applied to human affairs. Until comparatively recent times it was commonly held that the communal control of power and the elimination of force or violence from human relations were important elements in civilization. It was even believed that these views were not merely utopian aspirations, but had in many cases been translated into fact. In the nineteenth century great changes had taken place in the distribution and control of power between individuals, between individuals and the community, and between groups and classes, and the use of force or violence by individuals or by the state had been eliminated from many departments of human life. For instance, in Britain and

82

several other countries the potential power of a physically strong man—even a husband—to impose his will upon a weaker individual had been rendered practically inoperative by social organization and "public opinion". By similar methods the potential power of the man with an axe, a sword, or an automatic pistol in his hand had also been made inoperative. The power of kings over their subjects, of aristocrats over commoners, of men over women, of governments over citizens, and even of employers over employed had been greatly modified or in some cases abolished, and the use of force to make the power operative had also often been modified or abolished. Most people believed that it was possible not only to control and modify the use of power throughout society, but also that of violence, and to do so effectively for an intelligent purpose. It seemed, for instance, to be undeniable that the use of torture and flogging as methods of "doing justice" had been abolished in some places, that in others it was no longer possible to be hanged for stealing a sheep, and that in others the utopian idea of abolishing the death penalty had been adopted without apparently increasing the number of murderers or of their victims. All these appeared to be examples of the successful abolition of certain uses of force as instruments of communal power.

These nineteenth-century changes in the social control of power and the use of force and the efforts to eliminate force from the relations between states, governments, and individuals, were closely associated with the theory and practice of democracy, liberalism, and humanitarianism. Democracy, if it is to work, requires that power shall be given a completely different position in the social system and that people shall have a different attitude towards it than is necessary under other forms of government. In authoritarian societies, no matter what their particular type, power is taken as the main element to determine social relations and organization, and force is relied upon everywhere to secure obedience. Government is a hierarchy of superiors over inferiors or masters over slaves ; society is a ladder of power in which those who stand upon one rung exercise power over those standing upon the rung below them and can compel obedience by force. The two pillars of society are authority and obedience and they rest on the foundations of power and force. The nature and articulation of democratic society are entirely different. No society can be democratic—and democracy will not function in it—unless it is based upon liberty, equality, consent, co-operation, and tolerance. Each of these five elements requires that in practice power and force are given a different place in democratic than in other forms of society. Take the much abused and misunderstood " principle " of democratic equality. The equality of democracy does not mean that every individual is equal or that we must try to make them all equal and the same. It means simply that for certain social purposes they must be treated as equal. But if the community or state treats two men as equal for social purposes, it may and often does withdraw from the one power which he exercised over the other either because he in fact possesses some extraneous advantage or because he had been treated as socially superior. The state, for instance, by making everyone equal in the right to carry arms or in the abolition of that right directly alters the distribution and use of power and eliminates the use of force from social relations.

Consider, too, the position of consent, co-operation, and tolerance in a democratic system and their effect upon the use of power. The theory of nineteenth-century liberal democracy was that the state should be a community of free and equal citizens co-operating for a common end—the common good. The means for attaining that end was a government chosen and controlled by the people ; the choice, control, laws, and decisions were to be made through the vote of majorities. The power of the state and communal force could only be used against individuals, groups, or classes as a sanction of the law or of decisions made in accordance with law. Here again the theory of social organization is radically different from that of the authoritarian state. The basis of the authoritarian state is authority and obedience, power to compel obedience ; that of the democratic state is consent and co-operation, and the more people co-operate by consent in a common purpose the less use there is of communal power and compulsion. In practice the difference becomes even wider than it is in theory. Much can be and to-day is said against the liberal democratic forms of government and society which have developed during the last hundred years in Britain, the Scandinavian countries, and Switzerland, to take a few examples. But if their practice of the art of government, particularly in the use of power and force, is compared with that of Germany or Russia to-day the democrat or socialist who believes in democracy really has no reason to be apologetic. The experience of the last hundred years has proved that democracy cannot work unless it is based in fact upon consent, co-operation, and tolerance, unless the use of power is largely atrophied by the custom of co-operation and consent, and unless the use of force as a social instrument of government or organization is largely eliminated. Experience not only proved this ; it also led to the thing being actually accomplished to a considerable extent in certain countries.

This is really a strong and important point and weak-kneed democrats who are intimidated by raucous dictators and their imitators ridiculing and abusing democracy may be advised to cling to it for support. Society in Britain and Scandinavia is to-day very far from perfect, and democracy in those countries is not perfect, but they have developed a type of government, imperfectly democratic, for which a good deal can be said. Their merits and their democracy have been proportional to the consent and co-operation and the abandonment of compulsion. Where there is real consent throughout the community to the making of law by a majority and responsibility of the executive to majority decisions, and when there is at the same time a sense of co-operation for a common end in government, it is no longer true in practice that power and force, even though they remain in the background as the ultimate sanctions of law and government, are primary elements in determining social relations. The use of power has been modified or sublimated, and the use of force normally eliminated, by co-operation and consent. This is not just theory ; the process can be observed making profound social changes in our own country and other equally imperfect democracies in the years before 1914. Take the simplest case of the criminal laws. The attitude towards them has changed even in my own lifetime. The ordinary man to-day does not obey the criminal laws because they are imposed upon him by the power and force of the state ; it is not the police force which prevents him from assaulting his neighbour or robbing him with violence. The reason why he does not break these laws is that 99 per cent. of them have his consent. And this is true to-day of every class in the community. But it was not true even forty-five years ago. In the year 1895 on a Sunday morning in summer my brother and I were deliberately knocked off our bicycles on the main road outside Brighton by a band of " roughs " and " held up ".  There were quite a number of spectators, many of them respectable bourgeois.  No one interfered ; they thought it, no doubt, " unpleasant " and " disgraceful ", but not unusual.  So did we, and we escaped eventually with the loss of two shillings and a bent handle-bar.  Such things do not happen on the Brighton road to-day ; or if they do, at very rare intervals, no one—to whatever social class he belonged—would consider the occurrence as ." not unusual ".

These things do not happen to-day on the Brighton road or in London, in Seven Dials and other districts where they were " not unusual " fifty years ago, not because the police force is more efficient and the power of the state more effective, but because neither the police force nor the power of the state are required to prevent them.[1]  They are still, no doubt, prevented by the criminal law, the police force, and the power of the state ; but they are now unusual, because the law is normally kept by consent in all districts and all classes.  The way in which in democracies consent and a sense of co-operation modify the use of communal power and eliminate force can also be seen in the realm of civil law and

---

[1] Fifty years ago the police force was in one sense more efficient· In certain districts of London, the police always patrolled in couples. The fact that this is no longer necessary confirms what is said above.

88

state action which has nothing to do with the maintenance of law and order. It is true that state control in the lives of individuals has enormously increased in the modern democratic countries, and many people treat this as an increase in the power of the state and therefore of the use of force by it. This is a superficial and purely formal view of human society and human relations ; if it were true, it would justify the liberal capitalist objections to socialism. But it is not true. Socialization of industry and the organization of social services by the state do not necessarily entail the subjection of the individual more and more to the power of the state nor do they mean that he must be regimented by force. It depends entirely upon whether socialism or statism is or is not combined with democracy. If the state or community or socialism or communism—which may be several names used for the same thing—is considered as an end in itself, then you will have an authoritarian type of socialist society in which power and force dominate the relations between the community, the government, and the individual. That is a society of socialist masters and socialist slaves. But there is nothing in socialism which makes it inevitably uncombinable with democracy. And if socialism is combined with democracy, you get a form of society in which the active element in social relations is not power and force, but consent and co-operation. It is, of course, to a considerable extent a psychological distinction, but nearly all the important political and social factors have in the end to be stated in psychological terms.

In the Scandinavian countries, where there ·is already a fairly advanced system of social democracy, and in Britain and other countries where parliamentary democracy has proved stable and successful, although there has been an enormous increase in social organization and regulation by the state, it is not true that the power of the state and the force behind it are important elements in the day to day running of the social machine. The ordinary Englishman or Dane, when social legislation is passed of which he disapproves, complies with it, not because he knows that if he did not, he would be fined or imprisoned or put into a concentration camp or beaten up by the police or storm-troopers, but because it is a decision taken under a system of co-operation to which he consents and in which he can, if he choose, play an active part. He regards the state in its social activities as vaguely similar to his co-operative society, his trade union, his professional association, or his golf club ; it is part of the necessary, often useful, but frequently exasperating, machinery of modern life ; it is not an instrument of power, but of social organization, the means of providing education, drains, or trams, of regulating trade or traffic. When his trade union or his golf club makes a rule or regulation, of which he may or may not approve, he does not regard it as imposed upon him by power or force, and normally he regards the laws and regulations of the state or municipality in the same way. Even the rates and taxes, which he loathes and may try to evade, are a kind of super-subscription to a super-union or super-club. This attitude, which is the normal attitude of the normal man in all the democratic countries which I know, may indicate a lamentable ignorance of the true nature of the state and of modern political theory ; yet, in my opinion, it springs from sound common sense which is the beginning of political wisdom and of civilization. It is only when people begin to use the state and government, not as instruments of power or patriotism, but as part of the drainage system, that they begin to be civilized.

There is one other aspect of the democratic system, as it actually works, which is worthy of attention. It works normally through majority decisions. In theory this means that in a country like Britain or Sweden to-day, the minority on any question is completely subjected to the power of the majority, and minorities are compelled by force to obey the will of the majority. This has always been treated by aristocrats and dictators from the time of the Greek tyrants to that of Hitler as a cause for abuse or contempt. Nothing, we are told, could be more ridiculous than this government by the counting of heads. Well, to govern by counting heads is a good deal saner and more civilized than to govern

by cutting them off, and if one has to be completely
subjected to the power of anyone, the history of
Europe shows that there is a good deal to be said for
choosing to be subjected to that of democratic
majorities rather than to that of aristocrats and
dictators. And there is another reason which makes
the crocodile tears of the authoritarians for democratic minorities a little unnecessary. In practice,
if the government really is democratic, the minority
is recognized to have rights. It has an absolute
right to tolerance, which includes the right to free
speech and the right to oppose the majority. That
means that in the actual working of government
and the state compromise and consent play a very
great part, and the more democratic the system,
the more it is dominated by compromise and consent. This is not theory, but actual practice, as is
clear if you compare day to day administration in
Britain, Norway, or Switzerland during the last ten
years with that in Germany or Italy during the
same period. This habit of compromise is admitted
by anti-democrats to be characteristic of British
politics ;[1] it is anathema to the communist and
fascist and it can be a cause for infuriated despair
to the enthusiastic democratic reformer. Yet there
is much to be said for it. For it means that co-
operation and consent are really acting as determining factors in government and social organization ;

[1] As a matter of fact, it is probably even more characteristic of
the political system in Scandinavia and Switzerland.

but if that be the case, power and force are to the same extent eliminated.

The statement of these facts with regard to democracy is not a digression from my argument. They show that it is quite possible for human beings to change their way of communal life and to build society and government upon consent and co-operation instead of upon power and force. It has actually been done within the national state on a considerable scale under the influence of democratic beliefs. The facts also show that the effort to prevent war through the League was part of this movement away from government based upon power and violence to government based upon consent and co-operation. For the League, as its critics and opponents maintain, was a deliberate and " rational " construction ; it was a deliberate attempt to control and reduce the use of power and force in international relations by applying to them the knowledge which the experience of nineteenth-century democracy has given us with regard to such control within the national state.

And this was, indeed, one of the causes of its failure, but not quite in the way in which its enemies would have us believe. The League was, as we have seen, part of the nineteenth-century movement away from power, force, or violence to law based upon co-operation and consent. The war of 1914–1918 had for four years reversed that movement ; it reversed the process of controlling, sublimating, or eliminating power or violence. Modern war entails the adoption of force and violence as primary elements in determining a vast number of human and social relations which at other times are regulated by discussion, compromise, " law ", or other non-violent methods. Four years of such a regime had a profound effect upon Europe's social and political psychology, and soon after 1918 it became clear that, as a result, post-war Europe was not going to return easily to the nineteenth-century attitude towards power, force, and violence. In many countries governments allowed private armies to fight one another daily in the streets of great cities. Dictatorships took the place of democracies. Pogroms became a recognized method of administration. Breaking of heads was substituted for counting of heads and the concentration camp for consent as the basis of the best political system. Change of government or of a government's programme or policy was effected or prevented by " massacres ", " purges ", executions, or political assassinations.

The failure of the League was only an episode in this development, which was itself the result of the habituation of the European for four years to the unrestrained rule of violence. It was not, then, an isolated historical incident, the casual failure of an academic dream brought up with a jolt against the hard facts of life. It was only part of this general historical process or movement away from government by co-operation and consent to government by force which can be clearly discerned in the period between November, 1918, and September, 1939. But this confronts us to-day with a terrible dilemma. It is to be presumed that the war of 1939 will, like that of 1914, end some time some day. When it does, the world will be in precisely the same position as it was in 1918—only, perhaps, more deeply bogged in it. If the declared war aims of Britain and France mean anything—and only the superficial cynic or the purblind ideologist will deny it— we are fighting Germany to-day in order to establish in Europe a system of international relations which it was hoped and intended to establish by the League of Nations. There is no sense in talking of German or Russian " aggression " or in resisting the Nazi Government because of its action in Czechoslovakia and Poland, unless we mean thereby to prevent in the future a recurrence of such " aggression ". How can we do that unless we establish a European system different from that of Herr Hitler, Signor Mussolini, and Comrade Stalin ? How can we do it unless the Europe of 1950 is really going to be different from the Europe of 1938 or 1913, unless a system of inter-state relations is established, not dominated by the power and force of states and the perpetual threat of war, but based upon law, co-operation, and consent ? In a word, how can you prevent war ? And what is your quarrel with Germany and Herr Hitler if you think it " right

95

or " reasonable " or " inevitable " that the relations
of sovereign, independent states should be determined by their power?—for the test of a state's
power is war.

There then is our dilemma ; it confronts everyone
in Britain and France who thinks that we were right
to call a halt to Hitler, to oppose his aggression at
the risk of war. Our action is criminally useless,
unless its object is to create a system of international
relations in Europe in which the wars of 1914 and
1939 would be anachronisms and virtually impossible. If the system based upon power and power
politics which existed prior to 1914 and was resurrected in the years 1925 to 1939 by the abandonment
of the League is again re-created at the end of this
war, the present war will have been entirely useless.
For Hitlers and aggressions are the inevitable result
of an anarchical international system in which the
relations of sovereign independent states are determined by their relative power and the test of power
and the instrument of national policy is totalitarian
war. But that means that, if we do not again create
the League system in order to prevent war, we shall
have to create something very like it. And we
shall, as in 1918, be attempting to create it at the
very moment which in an important point is least
favourable to its success, a moment when, through
months or years of war, the minds of all of us are
accustomed and tuned to force and violence rather
than to law, co-operation, compromise, and consent.

*War*

The generation which in 1918 and 1919 said
" Never again " failed and were disappointed.   It
is senseless for us to be fighting this war unless we
say continually what they said :  " Never again."
But if their failure and disappointment are not to
be repeated in this generation, it is essential that
we should be absolutely clear in our own minds
as to the tremendous difficulties of changing the
international system and of doing it at the end of
a war.   It is from the experience of the years 1918
to 1939 that we may learn our lesson.   The problem
is the problem of national and international power :
how to control national power internationally, how
to substitute a system of law, co-operation, compromise, and consent for power and force in the
relation of states, and how to make the transition
to a pacific system of this kind at the end of a
period of unmitigated violence.   In the next chapter
I propose to consider this problem and the failure
of the League in some detail.

## Chapter II

# POWER, INTERESTS, AND POLITICS

THE establishment of the League of Nations was an attempt to substitute for the old system of power politics a new system of inter-state relationship. The crucial difference between the two is to be found in the position assigned to national interests and power in each. The old system assumes that vital interests of states are in conflict ; there is no community of interests which makes it possible to base their relations upon agreement, consent, compromise, and law. Where, therefore, there is a conflict of interests and those interests are vital,[1] the government of each national state must be the

---

[1] A vital national interest should mean and in theory sometimes does mean an interest which involves the existence of the state ; in practice it has meant any interest which the government of a state considers important. It has always been assumed that interests which are " vital " to Great Powers are not vital to small states. This chameleon character of " interests " should be noted, for it will add to our difficulties when we come to consider what national interests really are. It is not only in international society that interests change their colour according to the individual, class, or group to which they are attached. For instance, it has often been assumed that it is of vital interest to class A that it should have, and to class B that it should not have, something, e.g. a grand piano. It has often frequently happened that, when in fact one class has lost and the other gained its grand piano or what not, it has proved barely to affect the interests of either.

98

sole judge of the appropriate method of protecting the national interests. There being no community of interests recognized as underlying the relations of states, there can be no " law " recognized as regulating the relations, particularly in cases involving, in the view of a government, " vital " national interests. In such cases, the government must be not only the sole judge of how to protect the state's interests, but also of all the " rights and wrongs " in any dispute which may arise concerning them. But when that stage in social relations and organization is reached, the result is inevitable : the ultimate arbiter must be power and force. If there is no recognized law governing the states' relations, and no recognized method of settling disputes and differences regarding their interests by agreement or compromise, the relations will be determined by power and the conflict of interests settled by force. Thus the wheels revolve inexorably in one direction : power the instrument of national policy and war the ultimate test of national power.

The new system established by the League was, it is true, revolutionary, and it may be suggested that, if Europeans want to escape totalitarian war, they must accept the necessity of a revolution in international society. Some people hold, as we shall see, that the League went wrong, not in being revolutionary, but in being not revolutionary enough. The League created an association of member states ; the association was of a type, not unknown in history, to which political theorists have given the name Confederation. In theory each state maintained its complete independence and sovereignty, although it accepted certain obligations as a member of the association.[1] The association and rights and obligations of its members were created by treaty ; the objects of the confederation were limited and defined in the treaty, in short and simple language, " to promote international co-operation and to achieve international peace and security ". The most important means by which it was proposed to achieve these ends were as follows :

(1) The member states bound themselves by certain obligations not to resort to war.[2]

(2) They bound themselves to respect and preserve against external aggression the territorial integrity and existing political independence of all member states.

(3) They instituted a regular procedure of judicial settlement or of settlement by other pacific means of all disputes or differences which might arise between the member states and they bound themselves to use those methods and international machinery instead of war.

(4) Each state bound itself to treat the resort to

---

[1] In practice the League system, if its obligations are carried out, involves a large renunciation of " sovereign " rights by its members, e.g. their right to make war or to be judge of their own case where national interests are in conflict. In practice, too, whenever the League system was resolutely used for the purpose of preventing war and resolving conflict, the curtailment of national sovereignty proved capable of wider extension than would appear from a mere reading of the text of the Covenant.

[2] Most of the member states subsequently signed the Briand-Kellogg Pact, by which they agreed " to renounce war as an instrument of national policy in their relations with one another."

war by any member state in contravention of the fundamental obligations of the Covenant as an act of war committed against all other member states, to sever trade and other relations with the aggressor, and to come to the assistance of the victim of aggression. These obligations created what came to be known as the system of sanctions and collective security.

(5) They accepted some vague obligations which were apparently intended to lead to disarmament and provide means of altering the *status quo* without resort to war.

(6) They agreed to place under the direction of the League all the existing inter-state organization for co-operation in common interests and in some directions, e.g. international labour legislation, they created new organization.

(7) For carrying out the provisions of the Covenant and the objects of the confederation they created a permanent machinery of international government : an Assembly, a Council, and a Court of Justice. The exact functions of the Assembly and Council were not defined specifically, but in practice the Assembly approximated to an international legislature and the Council to an executive body. It was, however, only an approximation, particularly in the case of the Assembly, for its power to legislate was limited by the provision that only a decision agreed to unanimously by all members represented at the meeting of the Assembly could be binding.

The difference between this League system and that of the period before 1914 is, as I said, primarily to be found in the position of power and national interests under each. Under the old dispensation in all important matters the relative power of states, with war as its test, determined their relations, and this was considered natural, right, and inevitable. National interests being assumed to be in conflict, governments relied upon national power to protect and pursue national interests *against* the rest of the world. This is another way of saying that national policy was the protection or pursuit of national interests by means of power, and under such circumstances it is true that, in the often quoted words of Clausewitz, war is both " an act of violence " and also merely " the continuation of political relations by other means ". And nothing could show more clearly the basic position of power and force in the nineteenth-century view of international politics than this idea that violence is only the continuation of political relations by other means. For it is true only under special conditions, only if political relations are determined by power and force. It is not true if political relations are determined by law and co-operation.

The idea of the League was to attack this system at its root. States agreed to rely, not upon national power and force, but upon law, " rights ", justice, and co-operation for the protection of national interests. There was no attempt to eliminate differences in power entirely from the determination of international relations ; what was aimed at was to eliminate force or violence and to control and sublimate power in the form of rights under a system of law and order. This is the way in which power has often been controlled and violence eliminated from human relations. There are many cases in history in which the power of an upper over a lower class has been freely exercised by the use of force, but has subsequently been, not immediately and completely abolished, but subjected to control ; in such cases some of the power may be abolished and some of it translated into " legal rights ". The economic power of the employer over the employed was similarly dealt with in the nineteenth century. So too the power of the government, governing classes, or the state over the individual has frequently been controlled, without being abolished, in the same way ; this is the characteristic process of democracy by which the power of the state or, more accurately, communal power, which has previously been exercised by means of force and violence, is translated into a system of law, rights and obligations, and justice. If such a system develops so that it works mainly through consent, compromise, and co-operation, power and force gradually atrophy and cease to be important factors in social relations. And it is not true, as many people now go about saying with obvious satisfaction, that such societies have never and never can exist, that they are imaginary and utopian. Whenever and wherever men have begun to struggle out of barbarism into civilization, a society with these characteristics has begun slowly to develop.

The method of the League was an agreement not to resort to war or not to use war as an instrument of national policy and to establish a procedure and machinery which are practically universal wherever among human beings social relations are regulated by law and order, rights, obligations, and justice, compromise, and co-operation, instead of by power, force, and violence. Such a system requires the existence of permanent bodies of two kinds : one which shall make the law and rules which are to regulate the relations, and a second which shall decide disputes in accordance with the laws and rules, the rights, and obligations. Such bodies were created in the League and they were adjusted to the existing conditions of international society. The member states bound themselves to use the machinery and procedure for the settlement of disputes, thereby submitting themselves to third-party judgment [1] and abandoning the claim to be judge in their own case—an essential rule in any society in which relations are not to be determined by power and force and interests are not to be protected and pursued by violence. But immediately there arose a problem which is not peculiar to the international society of sovereign independent states ; it arises whenever an attempt is made to control the use of power and to eliminate the use of force from human relations and to subject a society to the rule of law or of rights and obligations.

---

[1] The League in fact did not actually go so far as to make this rule universal, but it is the logical and necessary development of the League system.

## Power, Interests, and Politics

What is to happen if an individual or group of individuals break the law or the fundamental rules for the settlement of disputes and resorts to the use of force in order to impose his or their will upon other members of the society? This is not a new question which has suddenly confronted the human race in the twentieth century and in the relations between sovereign states. During many thousands of years, almost from the day when he exchanged the status of an ape for that of a human being, man has again and again and again had to face this difficulty, wherever he wished to substitute law, order, and co-operation for force and violence in social relations. It is one of the crucial problems of politics, upon which at every epoch, in the streets of Babylon and Athens or of Berlin and London, have hung the life and happiness of the ordinary man and the fate of civilization. In one form or another the same solution has always been applied, for in fact the human race has discovered no other, namely to place behind the law the power of the community, to resist by communal force the use of force by an individual member of the society. The League adapted to sovereign states the lesson of experience which had been learnt in dealing with the anarchy of the man-ape, the savage with a stone in his hand, the man with a bow and arrow, a club, or a revolver, city states, kings, aristocrats, robber barons, Popes and Prophets, capitalists, joint-stock companies, trade unions, generals and armies, civil servants, tribes, nations, and provinces. They adapted it by attempting to organize the power of the community of states in order to control the use of power by an individual state, so that if an individual state, in breach of the rule of law, resorted to force, it would be resisted by the combined force of all the other states.

Such was the League " system ". It contained, as we shall see, certain important imperfections, and these may or may not have been among the causes of its failure. It may be, too, that the human race is for reasons which at least ought to be discoverable, if they exist, totally unable to apply to the relations of sovereign states a system of law and order, and so to control national power and eliminate violence and war. One thing, however, is absolutely certain. Whatever mystery may attach to the sovereign state, there is no mystery about this particular political problem. If war is to be prevented, the power of the sovereign state must be controlled and subjected to the rule of law. And there is no known way in which this can be achieved, unless states renounce war as an instrument of national policy, unless they are prepared to make binding laws and rules regulating international relations and to make changes in the structure of international society to meet changing conditions, unless they create and use a procedure for settling disputes pacifically in accordance with law and justice, and unless they co-operate in the common interests and compromise where interests conflict. To say that is to say again that, if the old international system continues to exist, totalitarian war is inevitable, and, if war is to be prevented, a system like that of the League is inevitable.

I propose now to examine the reasons for the League's failure and the position of those who allege that there was something fundamental in its constitution and working which made and always must make a system of that kind a failure. For it is only by doing this that it is possible to learn whether we can or cannot at the end of the second war do anything to prevent a third. The following are the most important reasons which its severest and most learned critics have put forward for the " inevitable " failure of any international system on the League model :

(1) That a League system is utopian because it ignores the " reality " of power and of conflicting national interests.

(2) That a League system is bound to break down because it does not go far enough ; it is an alliance or confederation of states, each of which retains its sovereignty and independence ; such an alliance to prevent war has never succeeded and never can succeed ; only a federation in which the sovereignty of separate states is merged can be successful in preventing war.

(3) A League system cannot work effectively because it relies ultimately upon sanctions and

collective security. There are two forms which this objection takes and they are very nearly, if not quite, contradictory. In one form the objection really falls under (1) and is made by the extreme realists. They maintain that under a League system the enforcement of law and order and the prevention of war depend ultimately upon the realization of a would-be aggressor that, if he resorts to force and war, he will have against him the overwhelming force of the rest of the community of states. Every state must therefore really be prepared to treat an act of war against one state as an act of war against all and to come to the assistance of any victim of aggression. But this idea is " utopian " ; it implies a community of interests among sovereign states which does not exist. The other objection comes from the extreme idealist side. It is made by the extreme pacifists who maintain that sanctions and collective security mean that the League attempts to prevent war by war and to eliminate force by the use of force, and that this is both morally wrong and politically impossible.

(4) A League system provides no real method of making the changes in structure and in relations which are necessary from time to time in all changing societies. It attempts to base international society and international relations upon law and treaty obligations, but makes no adequate provision for changing the law or adapting the rights and obligations, created by treaties, to new conditions. A

state entering such a system finds itself, therefore, rigidly imprisoned in the *status quo*, for law and rights must always be on the side of the *status quo* and of those whose interest it is to keep things exactly as they are.  Instead of preventing war such a system actually increases the danger of it, for any state for which it is a vital interest to alter the *status quo* is left with absolutely no means of doing so without resort to war.  It should be noted again that in one form—but not in all—this objection really falls under (1).  It is often maintained that any attempt to base international relations on law, rights, and " justice " is idealist and utopian, because it inevitably makes existing conditions unalterable and ignores the supreme " reality ", national power. Under the old system war or the threat of war was the acknowledged method of effecting changes in international relations ;  change was therefore effected by power and so the form of international society was always determined by the supreme reality, power.  And it always will be, so that any attempt to establish a permanent state of things on a basis which is not power must be utopian and illusory, for power, in the guise of war, will break in and break through it.

Those who think a League system to be unworkable as a method of preventing war thus fall into four distinct classes and their objections must be considered separately.  Let us begin with those who maintain that it is utopian because it ignores the " reality " of power and of conflicting national interests. The view is widely held by statesmen or politicians and by historians and political theorists, and now owing to the failure of the League very large numbers of ordinary people have consciously or unconsciously accepted it as proved to be true by that failure. It is probable that the vacillating and contradictory policy of the National Government towards the League since 1931 was really due to the fact that those who controlled that policy were always at the bottom of their hearts convinced that a collective peace system was impracticable and utopian. In November, 1934, Mr. Baldwin, as Prime Minister, made the following statement on behalf of his government :

> It is curious that there is growing among the Labour Party support for what is called a collective peace system. Well now, *a collective peace system in my view is perfectly impracticable* in view of the fact that the United States is not yet, to our unbounded regret, a member of the League of Nations, and that in the last two years two Great Powers, Germany and Japan, have both retired from it. It is hardly worth considering when those are the facts.

This statement was made at a moment when an act of aggression by one member of the League against another was known to be threatening. If the League system was to be used in an attempt to prevent aggression and war, the question whether the member states would stand by their obligations under the clauses which bound them to collective resistance to unprovoked aggression was crucial. The British Government remained a member of the League and did not denounce those clauses, but the Prime Minister's statement was meaningless if it did not imply that he no longer held himself bound by the obligations of collective resistance. Yet less than a year later and a month before the threatened aggression took place, although the position of the United States, Germany, and Japan with regard to the League remained precisely the same, Sir Samuel Hoare, Foreign Secretary in Mr. Baldwin's government, made the following statement on behalf of the British Government to the League Assembly :

> In conformity with its precise and explicit obligations the League stands, *and my country stands with it, for the collective maintenance of the Covenant in its entirety, and particularly for steady and collective resistance to all acts of unprovoked aggression.*[1]

Sir Samuel Hoare's statement seemed to be in direct contradiction to the Prime Minister's statement of November, 1934, and it was understood to mean that the Government had reversed its policy of the previous year and were now determined to use the League system of collective resistance in an attempt to prevent war or protect the victim of aggression. The act of aggression, the invasion of Abyssinia by Italy, took place one month after the British Foreign Secretary's speech. Two months later Sir Samuel Hoare, together with the French

[1] The italics in this and the preceding quotation are mine.

Foreign Minister, M. Laval, produced the Hoare-Laval proposals. If these had been accepted, they would have given to Italy all that she asked for at the expense of Abyssinia. It was almost universally held that this would mean another complete reversal of policy, a return to Mr. Baldwin's policy of November, 1934, and repudiation of the Covenant and of the obligations of " collective resistance to all acts of unprovoked aggression ". But in December, 1935, Mr. Baldwin stood by the League and collective resistance and repudiated Sir Samuel Hoare, who in September, 1935, had stood by the League and collective resistance and had thus repudiated the Mr. Baldwin of 1934. Sir Samuel Hoare went and his place was taken by Mr. Eden, a " believer " in the League. It is unnecessary to relate in detail the subsequent history of our foreign policy, how Mr. Eden and his policy had to go, in their turn, to be succeeded by the appeasement policy of Mr. Chamberlain, the failure of the League, the destruction of Austria, Albania, and Czecho-slovakia, and the final turn of the wheel or circle which has brought us to war or " collective resistance " against German aggression.

It is certainly not unfair to describe this policy of the British Government as vacillating and contradictory ; it would be easy, and probably unfair, to dismiss it as dishonest. It is much more important and interesting to discover the reasons for its vacillation. The real reason, I believe, is that neither

Mr. Baldwin nor Sir Samuel Hoare, neither Mr. Chamberlain nor the great mass of the supporters of the National Government in the House of Commons, regarded a League system as a practicable method of preventing war and regulating international relations. To them it seemed to be " utopian " ; essentially a " paper scheme ", the creation of idealists and the hope of large numbers of ignorant electors who were " against war ". If you had asked them why they believed this, they would have given you a quite different reason—for instance, Mr. Baldwin's argument in 1934 that the League was " impracticable " because the United States was not a member of it. That is because very few politicians—Bismarck and Lenin were notable exceptions—state and even fewer are aware of the real reasons why they hold political beliefs and pursue a particular policy.

If you want to know why a system, like that of the League, for preventing war is utopian, you will find the explanation fully set out, not by the politician, but by the professor of politics and history. Human beings are rarely content just to accept the simple fact of their miseries, savagery, and stupidity. They have an itch to explain and interpret them, to find some fig-leaf of theory or philosophy to cover the nakedness of their own folly and cruelty, to show exactly why it was inevitable that they should rush down a steep place into the sea. There are always professors of history and politics ready to

supply the fig-leaves, theories, reasons, and philo-
sophies, to comfort the dead, the dying, the disappointed, and the crucified with the assurance that
nothing could possibly have happened except in
the way in which it did happen and is happening,
and that everything is for the best in the worst of
all possible worlds.

One of the best and most detailed explanations
of why a League system is utopian and " impracticable " is given in a book recently published, to
which reference has already been made in the
previous chapter, *The Twenty Years' Crisis, 1919–1939*,
by Professor E. H. Carr. The particular fig-leaf
which Professor Carr applies to the distressing
nakedness of history and politics is a distinction
between utopianism and realism. The utopian,
according to him, is not concerned with facts,
realities, or cause and effect in politics ; he thinks
only of principles, ideals, and ends. He does not
analyse a political problem, but propounds a solution
out of the blue, and believes that it must work,
because it ought to work. He says to himself and
to the world : " X is right, good, or desirable and
Y is wrong, bad, or disastrous " ; he then invents
a visionary scheme, based upon imaginary facts,
which, if it " worked ", would give us X and abolish
Y, and he assumes that it will work simply because
X is right and Y wrong. Political utopianism
is a kind of dream world of wishful thinking.
Nineteenth-century liberalism, free trade, inter-

nationalism, and the League all belong to it, and the shadows which have wandered through its Elysian fields include, according to Professor Carr, Adam Smith, Bentham and the Utilitarians,[1] Plato, Confucius, Robert Owen, Fourier, M. Beneš, Lord Cecil, and President Wilson.

It is easy to see what Professor Carr means by utopianism ; it is much more difficult to be clear about what he really means by political realism. It dates apparently from Machiavelli. It is concerned not with principles, ideals, or rights and wrongs, but with " realities " and facts. It is

---

[1] The dangerous absurdity of making these sweeping generalizations about the utopianism of past generations and their schools of thought might have been avoided by Professor Carr if he had read John Stuart Mill's autobiography with the attention which it deserves from the political historian of the nineteenth century. Mill was a Benthamite, a utilitarian, and one of the most distinguished free-trade liberals of the middle of the century ; he should therefore be a typical representative of the utopianism of that era to which Professor Carr traces nearly all our ills. In the fifth chapter of his autobiography Mill describes how about 1830 he came under the influence of continental thinkers who were in reaction against the thought of the eighteenth century. He gives an account of some of the ideas which he derived from them and among them he mentions these : " that all questions of political institutions are relative, not absolute, and that different stages of human progress not only *will* have, but *ought* to have, different institutions : that government is always either in the hands, or passing into the hands, of whatever is the strongest power in society, and that what this power is, does not depend upon institutions, but institutions upon it. . . ." This, it will be observed, is precisely the theory of power and politics which Professor Carr has discovered and which, in his opinion, explodes, not only the League, but Mill and all that Mill and the nineteenth century believed. Mill himself supplies a comment which explodes Professor Carr : " These opinions, true in the main, were held in an exaggerated and violent manner by the thinkers with whom I was now most accustomed to compare notes, and who, as usual with a reaction, ignored that half of the truth which the thinkers of the eighteenth century saw."

scientific, for it interprets history and politics in terms of cause and effect ; the realist has no place for ethical judgments in politics, for reality is simply what happens. In international politics, therefore, the realist is concerned with the realities of interests and power where the utopian only thinks about principles and morality.

A few words must be said about the general theory, before we consider Professor Carr's application of it to the particular phenomena of international relations and the problem of preventing war. The theory is really based upon the popular use of the words utopianism and realism. The ordinary man means by utopianism a visionary scheme which cannot be achieved and by realism a scheme which pays regard to facts as they are and is therefore achievable, and in this sense a utopian is merely a visionary and a realist is a man who pays regard to facts as they are. For ordinary purposes the distinction is useful, and in everyday life we recognize roughly the difference between the visionary and the realist, though even in everyday life every visionary is to some extent realist and every realist to some extent visionary. But Professor Carr is not merely making a rough and ready distinction between political schemes which cannot and those which can be achieved [1] ; he professes

[1] Professor Carr sometimes writes as if he thought, like so many people, that a policy is utopian simply because it *has* failed, i.e. that no policy which has not succeeded could have succeeded, and

116

to give us a severely scientific analysis and explanation of the historical and political processes in Europe during the last one hundred years. But his method is profoundly unscientific, for in the first place he uses terms, particularly "utopian", "realism", and "reality", in their vague popular sense, without accurately defining them, and in the second place the psychological analysis, upon which the whole argument hangs, is superficial and inaccurate.

It has already been pointed out in the first chapter that the attempt, which Professor Carr makes, to

---

that the fact that the League failed proves that it was utopian. This view is, of course, closely connected with the so-called Machiavellian view that "reality is simply what happens". But there is no reason at all for believing it to be true. To accept it you must also accept the most rigid and extreme form of historical determinism. Even so, the theory makes no sense and is valueless for purposes of practical politics, for it is clear that policies and schemes have often failed, not because there was anything in the policy itself which was impossible or "utopian", but because of an event accidental to the policy, e.g. the death of its originator. Were the policies of Henry IV of France not utopian when he was alive and they were successful, utopian after his death when a lunatic and a butcher's knife allowed his opponents to reverse them, and once more not utopian when they were again successful in the hands of a Richelieu? As a matter of fact, when Professor Carr is dealing with policies and statesmen whom he approves instead of with those whom he does not like, he shows that he is fully aware of this. Where he approves of a policy which has failed, as for instance Mr. Chamberlain's appeasement policy, he sees that the failure does not prove its utopianism, and in another book by him, *The Foreign Policy of Great Britain from 1918 to September, 1939*, he writes : "There is a common inclination in politics to take the deterministic view that any policy which fails was bound to fail, and should, therefore, never have been tried. The charge that British Ministers were the dupes of the Axis Powers should not be too lightly made." But if the collapse of Mr. Chamberlain's policy of appeasement does not prove that it was utopian, the collapse of the League does not prove that the League was utopian.

base a distinction between utopianism and realism upon principles, ideals, and ends is invalid. All statesmen who pursue any kind of consistent and long-term policy have principles, ideals, or ends, even when they say nothing about them, and it is therefore impossible to get a scientific or clear definition of utopianism and realism by stating or implying that the utopian bases his policy on principles and the realist upon facts. You get no further by substituting the word " morality " for the word " principles ", as Professor Carr sometimes does.[1] If you are thinking of history and politics scientifically and not in the nebulous, vague way in which they are discussed in newspapers or a railway carriage, and if you are making a scientific attempt to ascertain the causes which determine history, this distinction becomes meaningless. To say that the unification of Germany is " right "—which is a moral or ethical judgment—is politically indistinguishable from saying that the unification of Germany is good or desirable. The unification of Germany was Bismarck's political end, ideal, or principle ; it was based upon an ethical or moral judgment. It was not utopian as opposed to his realism ; it was an essential part of his policy. It was not " mutually incompatible " with power, for his judgment that the unification of Germany was

---

[1] For instance, in the following sentence he seems to imply that the distinction between utopianism and realism is to be found in " morality " : " Every political situation contains mutually incompatible elements of Utopia and Reality, of morality and power."

right or good and should be pursued was determined partly by his judgments about power, and so far from the " morality " of German unification being incompatible with power, it was on the contrary translated into actuality by power. Again, take the case of Hitler ; Hitler is always talking about morality and principles, rights and wrongs. The fact that Professor Carr or I think wrong what he thinks right, and vice versa, does not alter the fact that he is concerned with morality and principles and that they are an essential part of his thoroughly " realist " policy. According to Professor Carr, we should have to say that Hitler is a utopian in so far as he has ethical ends and a realist in so far as he uses power to attain them, and that the means, even though they attain the ends, are incompatible with the ends. There must be something very wrong with a theory and definition which lead to such conclusions.

It is worth while to point out that Professor Carr is led into this absurdity because he follows the loose, popular handling of words and ideas. It is true that there is a broad distinction which can be drawn between people who pay regard to " morality "—in the popular sense—and people who do not in their pursuit of ends and objects. Roughly the difference really is between those who think that the end justifies the means and act on that principle and those who think and act on the opposite principle. To act on the principle that

the end justifies the means results politically in the
pursuit of what is considered politically right or
desirable without any consideration of " morality ".
It leads to " ruthlessness " and the ruthless use of
power, for power always appears to be the shortest
cut in policy. It is power that the strong man sees
to be the sharpest sword for cutting all his Gordian
knots. This is the essence of Bismarckian strategy
and of the modern theory and practice of the
communist and fascist. And many people regard
the statesman who, in this way, pursues his object
or end regardless of " principle " or " morality "
as essentially a realist ; he thinks of " real " facts,
not of imaginary " principles ". If this is realism,
it is itself a " principle " and based upon morality,
for the judgment that the end justifies the means is
itself an ethical judgment. It is, in fact, a doctrine
of the most doubtful validity and, as a principle of
policy, when translated into practice, it has probably
caused more misery and evil than any of the many
other false beliefs which the muddled mind of man
has invented to justify his cupidity, barbarism, and
cruelty. Professor Carr confuses this kind of
" realism ", which is an attitude towards the use of
means in politics, with the kind of " realism " which
he contrasts with utopianism, and which is or should
be an attitude towards political ends. As was
shown above, there is really no difference between
his utopian and realist, as regards ends. All statesmen pursue political ends, objects, or ideals, because

they consider them to be good, desirable, or right. In so far as they do this they act on general principles or fundamentals or morality—or, at any rate, they think that they do.[1]  There is nothing here to dis-

---

[1] I am not here concerned with the extremely interesting and important question of why everyone, from the man in the street to the great statesman or great conqueror, pursues or thinks that he pursues ends, objects, or ideals, and acts in this way upon general principles, continually making moral or ethical judgments that X is right, good, or desirable, and that Y is wrong or bad.  The world might have been different to-day, if the Kaiser Wilhelm II had had different principles of national policy and more stable ideas of what he considered politically desirable, and it is possible, indeed it is probable, that his political principles and actions, as the ruler of some 50 million human beings and commander of the most powerful army in the world, were largely determined by the fact that he was born with a withered arm.  Stalin's beliefs with regard to the desirability of establishing communism and the means by which he is justified in establishing it are not uninfluenced by the fact that he spent a good deal of his youth in Tsarist gaols and that thirty years ago he was flogged unmercifully in a Tsarist gaol in Tiflis.  No one can read *Mein Kampf* without seeing that Hitler's social morality, his beliefs as to the political ends which should be pursued in Germany and as to the means which the statesman *ought* to use for attaining those ends, are largely determined by his experiences many years ago in the underworld of Vienna.  It is practically certain that none of these statesmen were or are aware of the extent to which such accidents of personal psychology have determined their political principles, policies, and actions.  It is only in the last few years that, thanks to the work of Freud, we are beginning to be dimly aware of the relation between the rational and the irrational in the human mind and therefore of some of the most important effects of individual psychology upon social and political history.  But the origin of a man's general principles and ethical beliefs cannot alter the fact that he has them, and even though you may be able to trace a man's belief that the Jews are a social evil to the fact that he was an unsuccessful painter, or another man's belief that capitalism or communism is a supremely good social system to the fact that at the age of three he fell in love with his mother, and thus prove to your own satisfaction that he and all of us are politically not rational animals, it still remains true that these people do have these beliefs and may at any moment act upon them—and that, after all, is a relevant fact which may profoundly affect the lives of millions of human beings for good or for evil.

tinguish utopianism from realism, and that is why
in the latter part of Professor Carr's book his attempt
to make a distinction of this kind completely breaks
down. But there is a real distinction between
statesmen who do and statesmen who do not regard
principles and morality as applicable to the means
by which they propose to attain their political ends.
You may, if you like, call the latter realists, but
they are not the imaginary and non-existent realists
described in the first part of Professor Carr's book.
And the whole of human history proves that more
often than not they are fanatical visionaries, who
are always going to create a new world or a new
Europe or a new France or a new Germany or a
new Soviet Russia or a new religion, whose object
is so noble or magnificent that every means can be
justified in pursuing it, and who end, after sowing
the world with a new crop of misery, in destroying
themselves and a good deal of the civilization which
had existed before they began their operations.

We can now consider the application of this
general theory of utopianism and realism to the
particular problem of international politics and war.
Professor Carr maintains that a League system was
utopian and bound to fail, because it was based
only upon general principles and morality and
ignored the two outstanding " realities " of international relations, conflicting national interests and
power. This utopianism of the League is represented by him to be only a part or particular

instance of the great utopian movement of the nineteenth century, democratic and free-trade liberalism. According to this view, free-trade liberalism maintained that there was a natural " harmony of interests " in the world of states, that " conflicting interests " are a delusion, and that in fact no one and no state can really gain by the infliction of loss or harm upon someone else or upon some other state. Originally applied to economic relations only, this doctrine was subsequently extended to the whole sphere of international relations and is the basis of the League idea and the League system. For instance, according to its critics, the League assumes that the " true " interests of no nation can be served by war and that therefore the prevention of war is part of the " harmony of interests " ; there is a community of interest in the maintenance of peace. The League, they say, concentrates its attention upon this alleged and non-existent community or harmony of interests and ignores the conflicting interests. In doing so, it ignores the factor, power, for power is the instrument of conflicting interests. But the harmony of interests is an invention or delusion, or rather it is always the assumption of those " prosperous and privileged " persons, classes, or nations whose interest it is to preserve the *status quo* and to represent those whose interests are in conflict with their own, the have-nots, as disturbers of the public peace and assailants of the common interests of the community.

But conflicting interests and power are the real
" realities " [1] of politics, and any system which
ignores them is bound to blow up in practice, because
what determines history and men's actions is not
general principles or " morality " based upon a
non-existent harmony of interests, but power used
as the instrument for resolving the conflict of
interests. That was why the League blew up at
the first touch of " reality ". It sought to establish
the beginnings of international government by the
internationalization of power, but " since independent power is the basis of the nation-state, the
internationalization of power is really a contradiction
in terms ".

Like all theories put forward by people as intelligent and as learned as Professor Carr, this attack
upon the idea and system of the League contains a
certain amount of truth. But the main question
posed by him, on which the validity of his attack
depends, can be stated simply, and the truth of his
theory depends upon the answer to that and not
upon irrelevant, though important, truths which he
strikes upon in the course of a long argument. The
question is this : Is there something peculiar in
states and their relations which gives to their conflicting interests and to their power a peculiar

---

[1] Professor Carr wobbles over this point. He sometimes writes
as if common interests were always unreal as compared with conflicting interests and that some peculiar " reality " attached to
power and conflicting interests. (What " reality " really means
in this sense, I do not know.) At others he does appear to allow
some " reality " to common interests.

" reality " and makes a harmony of interests or co-operation impossible as the general and permanent basis of international society? In other words, was the League utopian because it attempted to organize the society of states on a basis of co-operation instead of conflict, to control or eliminate the use of power and force as the instrument of conflicting interests, and to apply to the relations of states the methods of law, compromise, and conciliation and the organization of pacific settlement and co-operation which the experience of thousands of years of human government had proved practicable and effective in other spheres of communal relationship?

The question is a perfectly plain and simple one, and upon the answer to it depends, not only the important problem of whether Professor Carr or Professor-President Woodrow Wilson is right, but something even more important—the destiny of the human race. The destiny of the human race, at any rate in the distracted corner of the earth which we call Europe, will be determined by whether the nature of national interests and power is such that the relations of states must inevitably be based upon conflict and power and that therefore the conflict of interests must periodically be resolved by totalitarian war. But in order to ascertain whether this is the case we must know a little more about the nature of national interests and power than sweeping generalizations as to the " reality " of this and the

" unreality " of that. Let us look, therefore, a little more closely at the nature of these interests and this terrible " reality ", power.

We may begin by unceremoniously getting out of our way a point with regard to national interests of which Professor Carr and many other people make a great deal. According to their view, liberal free-traders, the advocates of a League international system, and internationalists believe in an essential " harmony of interests," i.e. that in fact, if people were rational, they would see that conflicting interests do not exist, and that " true " interests are always common interests. If this belief is really the basis of liberal democracy and of a League system, they are based upon delusion, for the belief, as stated, is absurd. It is possible to quote, and Professor Carr does quote, isolated statements of distinguished and undistinguished " international-ists " which would seem to support this charge that they are imbecile utopians. But it is almost always possible to reduce truth to absurdity by quoting an extreme and incautious statement of someone who was trying to expound it. There is, for instance, a sense in which the statement that " all men are equal " contains one of the most important truths for anyone who is concerned with the ordering of social and political relations, but it does not mean that everyone is born with the same coloured hair or the same intellectual capacities. Thousands of writers have quoted the extreme and incautious

statements of democrats to prove to their own satisfaction that belief in the complete equality of every
human being in every respect is the universal tenet
of democrats and the essential basis of democracy,
and, since such equality obviously does not exist,
democracy—such, for instance, as exists to-day in
Switzerland—cannot exist.

So too with this business of the " harmony of
interests ".  No sane internationalist who advocates
some such system as the League as a method of
preventing totalitarian war has ever really maintained the harmony of interests in the sense which
Professor Carr would foist upon him, namely that
there are no such things as conflicting national
interests and that all the interests of all people,
classes, and nations are identical, so that all that we
have to do in order to obtain perpetual peace is
to shut our eyes, beat our bombs into tractors, and
bed the lions with the lambs.   And even if they had,
and every " believer in " the League, from President
Wilson down to the most cretinous ignoramus who
took part in the " Peace Ballot " of 1934, accepted
this grotesque doctrine, it would be completely
irrelevant to the question whether a League system
is in fact impracticable.   Because, whatever else the
League may be, it is certainly not an organization
of states based on the hypothesis that all the interests
of all the states which are members are always the
same.   On the contrary, the essence of the League
idea is a recognition that the conflicting interests of

127

sovereign states are real and dangerous, so real and so menacing that, if we do not want civilization together with these sovereign states and the wretched individuals who are the state's subjects—which means you and I and even Professor Carr—to be bombed into barbarism or annihilation, then we have got to find some method other than totalitarian war of dealing with these conflicting interests. To show that a League system is impracticable, it is no good showing that Adam Smith or Professor Toynbee or some other imbecile utopian believed in the " harmony of interests " ; you have got to prove either that totalitarian war is the only possible method in the twentieth century of dealing with conflicting national interests—which may, of course, be the case—or that the League method of doing so is in some particular respect impracticable—which may also be the case—or both. But if you are to discover the truth in these difficult and complex questions, you must be much clearer as to the nature of " national interests ", conflicting or otherwise, than people who simply assert that the conflicting interests of independent states are " real ", so real that any system which attempts to deal with them by law, compromise, and co-operation, instead of by power and war, must be utopian.

Every age has its own political or social shibboleth. In the eighteenth century it was " rights ", in the nineteenth century it was " utility " or the greatest good of the greatest number ; in the twentieth century it is " interests ". The blessed or accursed words " economic interests " seem, in the mouths of many people, sufficient to explain, not only the whole of human history and the behaviour of classes, but the infinite complexities of the human mind and the strange antics of individual psychology. The idea that conflicting national interests have a peculiar reality which makes them incapable of human control or manipulation and " inevitably " determines the history of twentieth-century Europe belongs to the same category of thought or mystical hallucination. In these theories or doctrines interests are treated just as natural rights were regarded in the eighteenth century, as fixed and immutable " natural " elements in human society, hard facts or realities, like climate or navigable rivers or the sun and planets, and therefore causes whose effects upon history are naturally inevitable and outside human control.

The idea that there are interests of individuals, classes, or nations which have this kind of nature is a complete delusion.[1] This will become clear as soon as we abandon the method of sweeping generalization and examine a few actual instances of interests in relation to society and politics. Let us begin with

---

[1] It should be added that though the delusion is complete, it is yet based upon and conceals an important truth. This is true of the shibboleths of every generation. There was a very important social and political truth underlying the natural rights shibboleth of the eighteenth century and the utilitarian shibboleth of the nineteenth. There is a profound truth underlying the Marxian shibboleth of economic interests.

a simple case of the social interests of individuals in everyday life. In the rush hour of going home in London, you may often see ten or twenty persons standing on the pavement in the rain anxious to get into an omnibus which will take them home and which has only room left in it for half of them. Here there is obviously a conflict of interest; it is to the immediate interest of each to get in himself and keep the others out. There are two ways in which this problem can be and is dealt with. The would-be passengers either struggle and fight to get in or they form a queue, often voluntarily, and enter quietly into the omnibus in accordance with priority of arrival at the stopping place. This is just as much a social problem as that of preventing war, a problem of organization of the relations of human beings to one another under particular circumstances in society. In the first case it is settled by conflict and competition, in the second by the establishment of a rule or law and by co-operation. What happens to the interests of the various individuals under the two systems? In the first case the matter is settled by physical power or force, and the stronger and rougher the would-be passenger is, the more likely on the average it is that he will get in, i.e. that his interest will prevail. The conflicting interests and the power of the strongest man to shove his way in are here just as " real " as the conflicting interests of two states and the power of the stronger to impose its will upon the weaker. But the interests are not

fixed and unalterable social entities with a peculiar
reality of their own which inevitably determines the
social behaviour of the would-be passengers. On
the contrary, they are extremely fluid and unstable
factors which depend partly upon unalterable facts,
e.g. that there are more waiting passengers than the
omnibus can hold, partly on power, partly on ideas
in the heads of the would-be passengers, and partly
on the way in which the would-be passengers decide
to organize their entry into the omnibus. For even
if they fight to get in and the power of the strong
man prevails, it is highly probable that his interests
would have been better served by not fighting. If
the people fight to get in, those who want to get
out have to fight to get out, and if there is a fight
every time the omnibus stops, the delays will be so
great that the strong man may well find that,
though he was the first man to get in, he gets home
later than he would have done if he had " waited
his turn " and there had been no fighting. So the
custom has grown up of the conductor shouting :
" Let the passengers off the bus first, please ", and
of the would-be passengers forming a queue
according to priority of arrival—you may see them
doing it with lamblike and voluntary docility any
evening in London, though in some places you will
also see the old-fashioned scrimmage. And with
the change of system from conflict to rule and co-
operation there is a change in the nature of the
interests. The conflict of interests is still there and

it has not changed into a common interest. It is still the interest of twenty people to get a seat in a bus which can only take ten. But by altering the system of dealing with this problem, though the interests of the people concerned still conflict, the nature of their interests has changed profoundly. It is no longer to the interest of the strong man to fight his way in and he no longer thinks that it is ; his interest is now the same as that of the weakest female child, namely that the rule of priority shall be strictly kept and that people get in and out in the quickest and most orderly way possible.

I suppose that I ought once more to apologize for talking about such trivial matters as clerks and typists waiting for a bus in the rain, when our real subject is the world-shaking policies of a Bismarck and a Hitler, the interests of states and empires, and the fate of civilization. But I see no reason to believe that we shall learn the truth about empires, any more than about clerks and typists, by using words and language which we do not understand. When people tell us that there is a peculiar " reality " about the conflict of interests of independent states which makes it inevitable that they must settle the question of these interests by power and force, they are using language which I do not understand, and which I do not believe that they understand. There is no reason to believe *a priori* that a conflict of interests between empires is essentially different from that between typists or that the best way of dealing with the one may not be also the best way of dealing with the other. Of course, this *may* not be the case. That is what I am trying to discover. But in order to discover it, you have got to analyse the nature of interests and conflicting interests, which Professor Carr and his school of thought do not do.

The typists standing in the rain have in fact already shown us something about the nature of " interests " which seems to me of some importance. Whichever of the two systems of dealing with the social problem is adopted, whether it is conflict and the use of power or rule and co-operation, the conflict of interest still remains so long as the original facts which gave rise to the conflict of interests persists—namely that you have room for only ten persons in the bus and there are twenty persons waiting in the rain. But though under these circumstances the conflict of interests persists, what it is to the interest of each person to do is different according to the system adopted for dealing with the situation. If the system adopted is conflict, it is the interest of the strong man to fight and use his power ; but if the system of queue is adopted, it is now his interest, like everyone's, to see that the queue is formed in the most orderly way possible. And it is obvious that that is what everyone in the queue believes, irrespective of his or her ability to fight their way in. A new " interest " has there-fore been created which is partly determined by the organization and partly by the psychology, by the beliefs in the heads of the waiting passengers. But it should be observed that there is, as a matter of fact, a third method of dealing with the whole problem and therefore with the conflict of interests. You might alter the facts which create the conflict. You might double the number of omnibuses. In that case there would be room for all and you would have actually removed altogether the conflict of interests.

Let us now leave the clerks and typists standing in the rain and go on to a more dignified instance. Let us examine the nature of the " economic interests " of classes under what is known as the capitalist system. When Marx formulated his theories, capitalism was pre-eminently a competitive economic system, and competition is the economic form of conflict. Capitalist competed with capitalist, trader with trader, and manufacturer with manufacturer. The system worked on the capitalist side through conflicting interests, and the conflict was settled by economic power ; victory and the reward of victory, profits, went to the economically strong. This white war between the rival capitalists, manufacturers, traders, and financiers has received less attention than the red war of Marxism, which is now known simply as the class war.

The Marxian analysis of the class struggle, as it existed when he and Engels studied the capitalist system, is irrefutable. There was an essential conflict of economic interests within the system between the capitalists or owners of the means of production and the workers or those who had no capital or control over the means of production. That conflict was resolved by power, and Clausewitz, if he had written about economics instead of military strategy, would have said that strikes and lock-outs are nothing but the continuation of economic relations by other means. And there was not only a conflict of interests between employer and employed, there was, so long as the system was carried on by unregulated competition, a desperate and bitter conflict of interest between worker and worker. In fact, the power of the employer over the employed sprang partly from his control over the means of production which made it possible for him to force the worker to do unwillingly what he wanted him to do because the alternative was hunger or starvation ; [1] but it also sprang partly from the conflict of interest between worker and worker. For over and over again, the unorganized workers are in exactly the same position as the typists waiting for the omnibus ; if there are twenty unemployed and only ten jobs, there is a conflict of interests between the unemployed, and if they fight one another for the jobs, it is the employer who rejoices, for his power over the worker is increased.

The world has changed since the middle of the nineteenth century, and profound changes have

[1] See p. 14.

taken place in the capitalist system, many of which were not, and could not have been, foreseen by Marx and Engels. They have had their effects upon the various conflicts of interests between and within classes. I shall deal with them in a moment, but before doing so it will be convenient to consider the system of communism or socialism which in the nineteenth century Marx and others urged should be substituted for capitalism as the method of regulating the economic relations between classes and of producing commodities for consumption by the community. People who in the middle of the reign of Queen Victoria maintained that socialism could be and should be substituted for capitalism were doing in the sphere of economic relations almost precisely the same thing as those are doing to-day in the sphere of international relations who maintain that a League system should be substituted for that of power politics and totalitarian war. Their object was to get rid of the conflict of economic interests and of the miseries and "injustices" inflicted upon the economically weak by the unrestricted use of their power by the economically strong. The system proposed by them aimed at doing this and dealing with the conflict of interests in two ways. In the first place it altered the conditions, the facts, which produced the conflict, and aimed at creating new conditions in which the conflict would no longer be possible. By transferring the ownership of the means of production from the individual to the community, it changed the distribution of economic power between classes and abolished the power of the employing class over the employed. It thereby abolished the fundamental conflict of interest within the capitalist system by abolishing the capitalist. But it aimed at doing something more ; it aimed at substituting co-operation and regulation for conflict and individualist competition throughout the economic system. The community or state would control production, and the whole system would be based upon co-operation to produce what the community needed, and not on competition to earn a profit or a wage or to find a job. It should be noted that the *possible* methods of dealing with these great economic interests of classes, which according to most people have been among the greatest formative causes of nineteenth- and twentieth-century history, are precisely the same as we found to be applicable to the infinitely unimportant conflict of interests in a group of twenty persons trying to get into an omnibus. The possible methods are three, and of these the second and third can be combined. The first method of resolving the conflict is by conflict ; you can fight until the stronger overpowers the weaker. The decision here is left to the naked use of power. In the case of the omnibus the passengers fight to get in and on the average the physically strong will get in and the physically weak will remain in the rain. In the economic system there will be unregulated competition between capitalist and capitalist, between worker and worker, and between capitalist and worker. Here the conflict will be resolved by economic power ; the economically strong will prevail and the economically weak will go to the wall. On the average therefore the economically strong capitalist will prevail over the economically weak capitalist, and as between capitalist and worker, the economic power of the former being infinitely greater than that of the latter, the interests of the capitalist will prevail over those of the worker.

The second method of dealing with the conflict is to alter the conditions which create the conflict. In the one case this is what you do if you double the number of omnibuses—you have created new conditions in which the conflict of interests no longer exists. In the other case, if you abolish the capitalist, you abolish the economic competition and therefore the conditions which created the conflict of economic interests.

The third method is to substitute for the system of competition or conflict a system of co-operation based upon law, rules, or regulations. You can do this either in combination or not in combination with the second method, i.e. you can leave the actual conditions which create the conflict of interests as they are and substitute regulated co-operation for conflict, or you can both alter the conditions, thereby abolishing the original conflict, and then substitute a system of regulated co-operation. The passengers who formed the queue left the conditions as they were, but altered their social relations, their interests, and the method of solving the social problem by stopping the fight and establishing a system of co-operation in accordance with a general rule or regulation. The socialist solution for the economic system, if it were adopted completely, would abolish the conditions creating the conflict of interests and would then create a planned economic system based upon co-operation for the production of commodities instead of upon competition.

But even in the economic system it is possible to apply the third method without the second, and this has in fact been done on a very large scale since the time of Marx and has caused those profound changes in the structure of capitalism which he could not have foreseen. Before examining them, however, there is one general point which may be noticed as highly relevant to the purpose of this analysis. It is significant that, as soon as socialists began to criticize the existing economic organization in the first half of the nineteenth century, to point out the evil effects of unregulated economic conflict, and to propose the substitution of a socialist for a capitalist system, they were met by precisely the same objection which Professor Carr and the critics of the League make to the idea of a League system of international relations. Some people, like Guizot, thought that socialism was abominable and socialists a menace ; others, like John Stuart Mill,[1] thought that there was much to be said for socialism as an " ideal." But all of them were agreed upon one point, and that was that socialism was completely utopian. All kinds of reasons were discovered which proved that capitalism was based upon eternal social " realities " and that it was utopian to imagine that you could establish a " system ", based upon abstract principles instead of upon facts, which would give the control of industry to the community and substitute co-operation for the conflict of economic interests. That conflict of interests was itself a " reality " which made a competitive system like capitalism inevitable—just as to-day, we are told, the conflict of national interests makes the power-war system of international relations inevitable. And the institution of private property was regarded in exactly the same way as the institution of the sovereign, independent state is to-day regarded by Professor Carr and so many other people, as something fixed and immutable, so that any attempt to alter it was not merely utopian and impracticable, but a " contradiction in terms ". Professor Carr can write to-day : " To internationalize government in any real sense means to inter-

[1] " Their (the socialists') aim seemed to me desirable and rational, however their means might be inefficacious ; and though I neither believed in the practicability, nor in the beneficial operation of their social machinery, I felt that the proclamation of such an ideal of human society could not but tend to give a beneficial direction to the efforts of others to bring society, as at present constituted, nearer to some ideal standard." *Autobiography*.

140

nationalize power ; and since independent power is the basis of the nation-state, the internationalization of power is really a contradiction in terms." If these sentences were translated into terms of private property and economic power, they would have had the enthusiastic approval of the vast majority of people in 1850, and they would have run somewhat on these lines : " To socialize industry and production in any real sense means to socialize economic power and abolish private property ; and since individual economic power and private property are the basis of society, the socialization of economic power and property is really a contradiction in terms."

The world is still by no means agreed as to whether socialism is or is not a desirable economic system. But no one to-day—except perhaps one or two extreme backwoodsmen in Piccadilly Clubs—would say that it was utopian or a contradiction in terms. For in fact the socialist system has superseded the capitalist system to some extent in all the highly industrialized countries of Europe, and even the most passionate realist cannot go on for long calling a system utopian or a contradiction in terms when it is operating over the greater part of the habitable globe and actually provides him with many of the goods and services which he regards as necessaries of life. This does not, of course, prove that the League critics are wrong in thinking that a League system is utopian. The fact that the conflict of economic interests and the rights of property, as they existed in 1850, have not proved the immutable realities which they appeared to be to contemporaries does not prove that the conflict of national interests and the independence of national states are not in 1940 the immutable realities which they appear to be to Professor Carr. But the fact is none the less relevant and important, for it shows that one must hesitate to accept sweeping statements about interests, conflict of interests, and power being such immutable social or political " realities " that they " inevitably " determine the structure of society and make any attempt to alter it or them utopian. Before we can agree that conflicting national interests and national power make the existing system of international relations inevitable and a League system impossible, we shall require some proof that the interests and power of nations have some peculiar characteristics which make it impossible to alter or control them in the way in which interests and power have been altered and controlled in other parts of human society.

I must now return to the question of those other changes in the structure of capitalism and the nineteenth-century economic system, the consideration of which I postponed. They were methods of dealing with the conflict of interests similar to those adopted by the passengers who formed the queue, i.e. the conditions creating the conflict were not abolished (as they would be by the substitution of

142

socialism for capitalism), but methods of regulated co-operation were substituted for unregulated conflict. There is no need to deal with this subject at any length, for the facts are notorious. Although the system of competitive capitalism was never formally abandoned or the system of socialism adopted, in all the highly industrialized countries of the world, between 1850 and 1940, methods of regulated co-operation were substituted for unregulated conflict again and again in such a way that many of the conflicting interests disappeared and power was controlled or eliminated. The result, in fact, has been that in most countries to-day the economic system is a bastard, half capitalist and half socialist, partly based upon conflict and partly upon regulation and co-operation. Mr. Durbin, in a recent book, *The Politics of Democratic Socialism*, says that the economic system of Britain is now " State-organized private monopoly capitalism ". This description indicates two of the major changes which have taken place since the time of Marx. As between capitalist and capitalist, monopoly has taken the place of competition, i.e. an extreme form of regulated co-operation has been substituted for the competitive system, which was thought to be the inevitable basis of capitalism. As a result, although the conflict of interests between capitalist and capitalist may still exist, they themselves are, like the passengers in the queue, no longer aware of it. At any particular moment it may be still the

143

immediate interest of the most powerful member of a trust or cartel to compete against his weaker associates or possible rivals—the conflicting interest is still a " reality "—but he is no longer aware of it ; he now regards his interest as the common interest that the terms of the trust or cartel or of the price and production regulating agreements shall be strictly kept or enforced.   In other words, a system of regulated co-operation in common interests of products has been substituted for one of conflict in which power determined whose interest should prevail.   The change from conflict to co-operation is the effect of a change in psychology,[1] in the beliefs of individual capitalists regarding their interests, but once it has come, the new system itself creates a new capitalist psychology, the psychology of co-operation in place of the psychology of conflict.

But there has been another major change in the economic system of Britain since the time of Marx. Besides the change from competitive to monopoly capitalism, there has also been the change from unregulated private capitalism to state-organized private capitalism.   This process by which the

---

[1] I do not mean, of course, that psychology is the only cause of the change.   In all social or political events—including social or political change—there are almost always two main factors operating as causes :  (1) Facts, i.e. that a certain situation has been created by events and actions in the past.   Among such facts economic causes are nearly always of the first importance.   Another series of facts usually of equal importance is that which determines the existing distribution of power.  (2) Psychology, i.e. men's beliefs and aims, what they believe to be true and what they desire or believe to be good.

144

*laissez-faire* capitalism of the nineteenth century has been gradually abolished by state interference, regulation, and control is too well known to require description. As a result the economic system has been semi-socialized. That means that the exercise of economic power by individuals and classes has been in part controlled or eliminated and that regulation and co-operation have often been substituted for conflict of economic interests. And these changes have been both the cause and the effect of changes in economic communal psychology.

Lastly the same process can be observed modifying the conflict of interests between worker and worker. Trade unionism does for the worker what trade agreements, trusts, and monopoly do for the capitalist. It substitutes regulated co-operation for unregulated competition. And the result has been exactly the same as with the capitalist or the passenger in the queue. The conditions which create the conflict of interests between worker and worker still exist in the economic system itself, and therefore the conflict of interests still exists wherever and whenever there are more workers seeking jobs than jobs seeking workers. But trade unionism has substituted for the actual conflict and competition a system of regulated co-operation in the method of seeking the jobs. And it has profoundly modified the conflict of interests by creating a new common interest in maintaining the trade union regulations.

We have now examined two examples of conflicting interests in social relations, one trivial and the other of immense importance, and in each case we have found that there are only three methods by which individuals or the community can deal with such a conflict : (1) It can be settled by conflict itself, by fighting the matter out, in which case the interest of the more powerful will prevail ; (2) The conditions which create the conflict can be abolished, in which case the conflict of interests will itself be abolished ; (3) A system of regulated co-operation can be substituted for the method of fighting, so that the conflict will be adjusted peacefully and with due regard to the general interests of the whole community. We are now in a better position for examining the nature of the power and conflict of interests of independent states. What we want to know is whether there is something essentially different in such national power and interests from those in the two cases already examined which makes it impossible to apply to them the second or third method described above. If there is no essential difference, then there is absolutely no reason for believing that some such system as that of the League is utopian or that power politics and war are inevitable. Even so, of course, it may still be true, not that the League was utopian, as established in 1919, but that it contained certain faults in structure or design which were responsible for its breakdown. These are the questions to which we must now devote our attention.

## Power, Interests, and Politics

Let us begin by asking a question which is practically never asked or answered by the practical statesmen or political theorists who tell us so much about the enormous importance and reality of national interests and power : " What are national interests and power ? " The answer with regard to power has been given in the previous chapter. National power consists of a large number of different factors, geographical, demographic, economic, political, psychological, etc., which make it possible or probable that the individuals who form the government or are the citizens or subjects of a state within a defined area will be able to make life so intolerable to the individuals who form the government or are the citizens of another state that the latter will against their will be compelled in the last resort to do what the former wish them to do. National power, like all power, belongs to and is exercised by individuals upon or against individuals. If the individuals are organized, the power can be organized, and national power is therefore the organized power of the individuals organized in a nation or state. To speak about national power as attached to or exercised by the " nation " or the " state " is to speak in metaphors ; the nation or the state is not an entity which can itself exercise power or against which power can be applied.

What is true of national power is also true of national interests. When we talk of the interests of " Germany " or of " Britain ", we are talking metaphorically ; there is in existence no entity, " Germany ", whose interests conflict or are in common with another entity, " Britain ". What we mean is that the individuals who form the government or are the subjects or citizens in a certain area have interests which conflict or do not conflict with the interests of individuals in another area. There is no doubt that this is true, although many people have got their minds into a muddled condition in which they cannot be brought to see it. It is another example of the disastrous results of the human imagination, to which reference was made on page 16. It is by our imagination that we ascribe a personality to Germany or Britain, but having done so, people forget that the thing is imaginary and begin to speak and talk as though Germany can eat and drink and fight and gain and be tortured and be put into a concentration camp or given a dose of castor oil. And it is a curious fact that it is the realists, like Hitler and Professor Carr, who are shocked by anyone being so utopian as to believe that a League might work, who are also most prone to endow states and nations with an imaginary personality and then to believe that it is " real ". But it is not real, it is purely imaginary. Neither Germany nor Poland nor Czechoslovakia has a stomach or a body or a mind or a soul ; that is why they cannot eat or drink or be tortured or rule or have power or interests. It may be true that the interests of the Germans conflicted with the interests of the Czechs, and that therefore the Germans destroyed the state of Czechoslovakia ; it is not true that the interests of Germany conflicted with those of Czechoslovakia. That this is the case can be seen in the fact that the destruction of Czechoslovakia was accomplished by the acts of individuals against individuals, and that now, though Czechoslovakia no longer exists, it is individual Czechs who suffer the consequences, and the interests of the unfortunate individual Czechs still conflict with the interests of individual Germans who exercise power over them.

This may sound elementary, primitive, and childish. I dare say it is, yet it is one of the most important of all political truths at the present day, and one which not 10 per cent of the population of Europe understand or believe. If 50 per cent of the population believed it and understood what it meant, there would certainly be no Hitler and probably no power politics or war ; there would be a League system working as efficiently and naturally as the L.C.C. or the N.U.R. ; and Professor Carr, instead of explaining to us the terrific reality of power and national conflicting interests, would be giving the most interesting lectures to his pupils in Aberystwyth on the utopianism of Napoleon, Bismarck, and M. Clemenceau, the reality of the League, and the inevitability of international co-operation in the modern world of closely knit international common interests. But they don't,

F

and so all this is " utopian " ; and they don't believe it because the misuse of the human imagination is socially and politically a curse and always has been. That is why in politics we reject the simple, homely truths which might make the world a decent and civilized place to live in, while we accept the totem-ism, the hoodoos, the ju-jus of Hitler and all the other medicine men of nationalism, and Professors of International Politics sit in their universities translating the magic formulæ of the statesmen into the abracadabra of " science " and so proving how right and how inevitable it is that we should all be engaged so often in trying to kill one another.

It is only if you give an imaginary personification to states and then induce yourself to believe that the personification is somehow or other not imaginary and the states have a real existence and personality apart from the individuals which compose them that you can also accept the false belief that states have interests and power, fixed, immutable, endowed with a peculiar reality which makes it inevitable that their conflict of interests must be resolved by power and utopian to think that their relations can be regulated by an orderly and pacific system of law and co-operation. For if interests and power attach, not to a personified state, but to the indi-viduals who compose the states and their govern-ments, it becomes clear that what we call national interests and power are interests and power attached to a group or association of organized individuals essentially of the same nature as the interests and power attached to a group or class of individuals such as capitalists or workers or trade unionists. As social and political factors, such group interests and power are not simple and immutable ; on the contrary they are extremely complex and, in many ways, unstable. They may be among the most powerful elements which determine the social action of individuals or groups of individuals ; but, although their effects upon society may be profound, their complexity and instability make it impossible to say that they must always remain the same and have one particular "inevitable" result. They are always factors which can themselves be modified, controlled, or even eliminated, and what effect they will have at any particular moment depends upon the way in which human beings regard them and deal with them. It is true that, more often than not, men have allowed themselves to be made the slaves of interests and power ; the whole of history shows that this is never necessary or inevitable and that, if they have the will and a little intelligence, they can be the masters of both and of their own souls.

That this is the case can best be shown by comparing class interests under a capitalist system with national interests under a system of power politics and war. No conflict of interests could possibly be more intractable or "inevitable" than those of the workers and the capitalists if the economic system is organized as it was in the nineteenth century. And since the system itself was organized on a basis of conflict and competition, power was necessarily the determining and most " real " factor in the economic relations between individuals, groups, and classes. Yet, as we saw just now, these " interests " were not simple, fixed, immutable factors in society the social effects of which, as causes, could be predicted scientifically in the way in which you can predict the effect of hydrogen if you mix it in a certain proportion with oxygen. You cannot, for instance, say that the conflict of interests is such that it must inevitably under all circumstances be resolved by conflict and power.[1] On the contrary the interests themselves at any particular moment were extraordinarily unstable and fluid. Not only was there the " fundamental " conflict of interest between the capitalist class and the worker class, but the interests of some capitalists conflicted with those of other capitalists and the interests of some workers conflicted with the interests

[1] I say this, although I hold myself to be a Marxian socialist, and I do not believe that it is contradicted by the essential truth in Marx's own theory. The extreme neo-Marxist would, of course, deny the statement absolutely ; they regard the conflicting economic interests of classes as fixed and immutable social causes inevitably producing certain results and resolvable only by the use of power, in exactly the same way as Herr Hitler and Professor Carr regard national interests and power. And it is significant that, just as Herr Hitler and Professor Carr have to give to states a " real " imaginary personification in order to give their interests and power this imaginary immutability, reality, and inevitability, so the neo-Marxists in the same way personify classes in order to be able to ascribe the same imaginary qualities to class interests.

of other workers. Indeed it is notorious to anyone who knows anything about the actual working of the industrial system and of Labour organization that at any particular time or place there may be a group of workers whose economic interests appear to be the same as those of a group of capitalists or employers and in conflict with those of another group of workers.

The reason for this is that the economic " interests of the capitalist class " or " of the workers' class " are the interests not of an entity or of a person, but of the individuals who compose the class. It is the individual workers, not the class, who exist and to whom the interests, power, or lack of power attach. Hence though it is true that on the whole and in the long run there is a fundamental conflict of interests between the workers and the capitalists under the capitalist system, the interests and the conflict are at any particular moment fluid and unstable, and it is an imaginary and false simplification to speak and act as if all the interests of all the workers conflicted always with all the interests of all the capitalists. They do not, and moreover the whole matter is complicated still further by the fact that whether and to what extent the interests conflict depends partly on facts, such as the actual economic organization, and partly on the psychology, not of a personified class, but of the individuals in the class. The nature of the interests and whether there is or is not a conflict will be determined to a

153

considerable extent by what individuals actually believe to be their interests and what is the best way to settle a conflict of interests if it exists.

In consequence, as we have seen, the whole system —the interests themselves, the conflicts of interest, the use and possession of economic power, the economic and social relations between individuals and classes and between them and the community and state—were profoundly modified between 1850 and 1940. When the capitalists substituted co-operation for competition, they produced the monopoly system ; when the workers substituted co-operation for competition, they produced the trade union system. In both cases the " system ", the interests, and the conflict were changed, and they were changed, not because the interests had altered, but because the beliefs of individuals with regard to what their interests were and how a conflict should best be dealt with had changed. In some industries the system of collective bargaining between workers and employers and the working out of elaborate agreements regulating wages and conditions over a whole trade substituted some measure of co-operation for conflict even between the worker and the capitalist. From the other end, the enormous increase in state regulation and control, the fixing of minimum wages in certain industries and the establishment of Whitley Councils, changed the actual conditions which had previously determined the interests or the conflict of interests.

Finally, this process was immensely accelerated and increased by the continual encroachment of socialistic forms of organization upon those of private capitalism through nationalization and the economic activities of Local Authorities, Public Utility Corporations, and the Co-operative Movement. The capitalist " system " as Marx knew it is barely recognizable in the economic " system " of Great Britain to-day, and there is no reason, except superstition or perverted imagination, for believing that this process of substituting co-operation for conflict, of subjecting the unregulated use of economic power of individuals and classes to communal regulation, of transferring control and ownership in the economic system from the individual to the community, could not be extended, without violence or bloody revolution, until the capitalist system of power economics and " inevitable " conflict has been transformed into complete socialism, in which regulated co-operation in common interests has taken the place of conflict.

If you compare nation interests and power with class interests and power, bearing these facts in mind, you will find that the only essential difference between them is that the first belong to individuals organized in nations and the latter to individuals organized in classes. And you will also find, if you examine the facts of European history instead of the figments of your own imagination, that precisely the same processes have actually been operating in

national interests and power since 1850 as we have
seen operating in the capitalist system and among
the passengers waiting for the omnibus.  The idea
that there are fixed and immutable conflicts of
interest between nations such that they must
inevitably be resolved by power is disproved by
facts and by history ; over and over again in the
ordinary course of events and diplomacy, without
the intervention of any utopian President or League,
such conflicts have been resolved either by changing
the conditions which created them or by a change
in the national attitude[1] to them so that, though
the interests might still conflict, it was agreed to
deal with them by compromise and regulated
co-operation instead of by conflict and the use of
power.

Let us examine a few examples.  It is a curious
fact that those who insist that the nature of the
independent state is such that it must have conflicting
interests with other states and that the conflict
must be resolved by power always find their proofs
in the policy and demands of what are called Great
Powers, and of those Great Powers who attempt or
threaten to change the *status quo* by war.  It is as
though, in order to find out whether it is possible
to establish a government based on law and co-
operation in Britain, you confined your investigation

---

[1] And a change in national attitude is a change in the attitude
or beliefs and aims, not of a person called Germany or Britain, but
of the individuals who form the government or nation in Germany
or Britain.

156

*Power, Interests, and Politics*

solely to the long-term prisoners in His Majesty's prisons and ignored the psychology and behaviour of the remainder of the population as abnormal or unimportant. If the nature of the independent sovereign state is such that international government is not merely difficult or impossible, but "a contradiction in terms", and it must inevitably pursue its own interests against other states by the use of its power, this must apply no less to the smaller than the larger, to the less powerful than the more powerful state. It is no good replying that the small state has to sit still and do what it is told precisely because power is the main and ultimate determinant in international relations. That fact, of course, explains why under a system of power politics and war Luxemburg does not declare war on Germany or Finland on Russia ; if the international system is based upon conflict and power, the interests of Great Powers prevail over those of the small states normally without the actual use of force. But it does not explain why the relations of small states to one another are not determined by power and the conflict of interests.

In the north of Europe there are five small states who may be said to be neighbours : Norway, Sweden, Denmark, Holland, and Belgium. In the south of Europe there were also five neighbouring small states : Serbia, Bulgaria, Rumania, Greece, and Turkey. During the last sixty years there is only one solitary case in which a major conflict

157

of interests developed among these northern peoples,
the demand of the Norwegian people for separation
from Sweden. That conflict was of a kind which,
again and again since the Napoleonic wars, has
resulted in war ; the Swedes and Norwegians settled
it without the use of power or war by agreement
and co-operation. In all other cases, too, these
five states have for sixty years relied solely upon
agreement, compromise, and co-operation, and it
is impossible to see that relative power had any
effect at all upon their relations. The history of
the five small states of south-eastern Europe was the
exact opposite. The Balkans became a byword for
conflicting national interests and " balkanization "
came to mean simply a system of small states whose
relations were based upon conflict and war or the
threat of war.

What is the reason for this extraordinary difference ? There is no evidence for thinking that by a
dispensation of God or geography the interests of
independent states in south-eastern Europe habitually conflict while those of independent states in
north-eastern Europe are always in common. If
conflicts of national interest and power must
inevitably determine the relations of states and this
accounts for the fact that Germany and France have
fought one another three times since 1870, it is
extremely mysterious that Belgium and Holland,
which have common frontiers with each other and
with the two Great Powers, have never during the

same period been anywhere near war and that there
is no sign of power or conflicting interests having
had any vital influence upon their relations. It is
the more mysterious (and at the same time illumin-
ating) if one remembers that little more than a
hundred years ago the Dutch and Belgians fought
each other in a war which lasted from 1830 to 1833.
The interests involved in that war were those of
nationalism, which has been the apparent cause of
nearly all the Balkan and European wars of the
last century. They were precisely the same interests
which were the subject of the major dispute, referred
to above, which arose between Swedes and Norwegians in 1905. The European autocrats of the
Great Powers who constructed the new Europe of
1815 after the Napoleonic wars joined together the
Swedes and the Norwegians in one state and the
Dutch and Belgians in another without consulting
the inhabitants. In the one the Swedes and in the
other the Dutch were the senior partners who
gained, or thought that they gained, by the union.
From the first the Belgians and Norwegians were
dissatisfied and wanted " independence ". In 1830
the Dutch-Belgian dispute was settled by war and
power ; in 1905 the Swedish-Norwegian dispute
was settled without war by agreement ; the result
of both settlements was exactly the same, Belgium
was separated from Holland and Norway from
Sweden. And there is no evidence that after the
settlements conflicting interests and power have had

any importance in determining the relations of either Holland and Belgium or Sweden and Norway.

I have said that these facts are mysterious. They are mysterious, indeed they are totally inexplicable, if you adopt the theory of history and international relations which describes men and women and " states " in metaphors and then delude yourself with the belief that your metaphors have " real " existence. But there is no mystery and nothing inexplicable in all this if you stick to the simple and somewhat silly facts which determine human relations both in the nightmare of European history and on the solid pavements of the London streets. Of course, all the interests of all the Belgians or Swedes are not the same as all the interests of all the Dutch or Norwegians. Of course there are conflicting national interests between the states of north-eastern Europe just exactly as there are between those of south-eastern Europe. Of course there was a conflict of interests in the demand of the Norwegians for independence and in the demand of the Belgians for independence. And of course conflicting interests and power are just as important or unimportant factors in determining the relations of all these small states in the Balkans or in Scandinavia as in determining the relations of Great Powers.

The explanation of the difference in the effects of apparently similar causes in these several cases is to be found not in the nature of national interests and power, but in the different attitude of human beings towards such interests and towards power as a method of resolving conflict. The Balkans between 1900 and 1914 were a hotbed of what we call nationalism ; Serbs, Bulgarians, Rumanians, Greeks and the other national segments of humanity took the view of international relations now held by dictators and the Professor of International Politics in the University College of Wales. They believed that they had irreconcilable interests which could be settled only by power. And because that was the way in which they regarded their interests, their interests were, in fact, irreconcilable. Like the passengers struggling to enter the omnibus, they made uncontrolled use of power the arbiter of their interests ; they resolved the conflict of interests by conflict, by fighting it out. Their attitude and their actions were the same as those of France and Germany since 1870. The Swedes and Norwegians in 1905 and the small states of northern Europe since 1833 have acted on a different system. They have not been so foolish as to believe that all their interests are always harmonious. But like the omnibus passengers who form a queue, their attitude has been that the best way of settling a conflict of interests is, not by conflict and unregulated power, but by agreement, compromise, and regulation. According to Professor Carr, we must say that the policy and methods of the northern states have been " utopian ", while those of the Balkans and

France and Germany have been " realist ". If we
are to judge by results, it is a little difficult to see
where exactly realism is superior to utopianism in
international relations. The ordinary man in Scandinavia, Holland, or Belgium is just as good a patriot
as he is in Yugoslavia, Bulgaria, or Greece, and all
the evidence points to the conclusion that in the
long run the northern peoples and states have one
and all gained enormously by settling their differences by compromise and regulated co-operation,
and that in the Balkans neither peoples nor states
have gained anything over them by fighting it out.
The proof of even an international pudding must
be in the eating ; most people would agree that the
condition of Scandinavia, produced by the one
method of international cookery, was immeasurably
superior to that of the Balkans, produced by the
other method.

In the previous pages and example we have been
dealing with small states. " Ah," we shall be told,
" you are one of those incorrigible utopians of the
Wilson school who think you can put the small
state on the level of the Great Power. Of course,
the small state has to settle its goose or pudding
as best it may without the use of power. In fact,
that is an additional proof of the overwhelming
importance of conflicting interests and power in the
relations of the Great Powers. You cannot compare
the relations of Holland and Belgium with those of
Germany and France or—remember ' the scrap of

paper '—of Germany and Belgium. Even a League
system may work where unimportant interests are
at stake or in disputes between the smaller powers.
It is in the major conflict of the major interests of
Great Powers that power must be the ultimate
arbiter and therefore a League system is utopian."

I shall examine the case of the Great Powers in
the same way as I have examined that of the small
states, in order to test the validity of this objection.
But before doing so, there is one point in connection
with it which deserves attention. The examples
which have been examined, although they refer
only to small states, have at least knocked one or
two considerable holes in the theory that conflict of
interests and power make a League system impossible. First they show that, as between small
states, there is nothing which makes national
interests and power essentially different from the
interests and power of other organized groups of
individuals. The state does not cease to be a state,
sovereign and independent, merely because it is
relatively small or not " Great ". We have seen
that in actual practice there have been two entirely
different systems of regulating the relations of these
sovereign, independent states and of dealing with
their conflicting interests : (1) the unregulated use
of power or force and war ; (2) compromise, rule
of law, and regulated co-operation. There is therefore nothing in the nature of the sovereign, independent state which makes the first system inevitable

163

and the second impossible, i.e. which makes power the inevitable instrument of state action and therefore the determinant of international relations.[1]  It follows that if power must inevitably determine international relations and conflicts of national interests and is internationally uncontrollable, the cause is not to be found in the nature of the sovereign, independent state, but merely in the largeness or power of some states.

Let us leave the waters where swim the smaller fry and boldly enter the mighty depths of high policy frequented by these Great Powers.  The international relations of two of the greatest of them, France and the British Empire, between 1895 and 1940 throw light on the real nature and effects of national interests and power.  It will not be disputed that in 1895 France and Britain—the French and British people—had a large number of conflicting and a large number of common interests.  This had also been the case throughout the eighty years which separated 1895 from the Battle of Waterloo and the Treaty of Vienna.  During that period the general policy of the two countries towards each other had vacillated between " friendliness " and hostility.  At times, as in the thirties and during the Crimean War, their governments discovered that their common interests were the

[1] This is, of course, implied in the statement of Professor Carr, already quoted, that " since independent power is the basis of the nation-state, the internationalization of power is really a contradiction in terms ".

stronger and would best be served by close co-
operation. But this state of affairs was exceptional ;
throughout the greater part of the period it was
generally assumed that the major interests of France
and Britain, particularly in the sphere of economic
and imperial expansion, were irreconcilable and
that ultimately they must be determined by power.
The armaments of Britain were always prepared
on the assumption that they would have some day
probably to be used against France and Frenchmen
when the conflict of national interests " inevitably "
was resolved by the test of national power. For
instance, in 1858 there was a naval scare which
was almost exactly the same as the " We want eight,
and we won't wait " scare of 1909, but in 1858
the enemy was France and in 1909 it was Germany.
The volunteer movement was the result of the earlier
scare ; it was directed against France, was encouraged by Palmerston, " one of the greatest nineteenth-
century advocates of ' preparedness ' ", and was
enthusiastically supported by the British public
which at the time suffered " from dreadful visions
of French battleships and transports stealing across
the Channel in the dark, and conveying hordes of
French soldiers who thirsted to indulge their
instincts for rapine on English homes ".[1]

Between 1890 and 1900 this traditional policy,
based upon conflicting interests and power, governed

[1] The quotations are from *Lord Palmerston*, by Herbert C. F. Bell,
vol. II, pp. 237 and 238.

the relations between Britain and France. The governments of the two countries conducted their foreign policy on the basis and hypothesis that the most important, the " real ", interests of France and Britain were in conflict, and that their common interests were unimportant or illusory, the utopian hallucinations of little Englanders and pacifists. What benefited France harmed Britain, and vice versa twice over. Their international relations were therefore necessarily dominated by the conflict of interests, and the main instrument of policy was power. Co-operation, compromise, political machinery for composing differences or pursuing common interests were, in all matters of " vital interest " or of " honour ", ruled out as utopian or unpatriotic ; on both sides of the Channel statesmen thought of the use of (or threat of using) power, economic or military, to promote the interests of their own country at the expense of the other as the proper and inevitable instrument of policy. The result was that the ultimate test of power, war, very nearly came on more than one occasion. The conflict of interests over their possessions on the Niger river in Africa actually produced fighting between French and British, and war between the two countries over this question seemed to be imminent in March, 1898. Most historians have forgotten this, but even they record the Fashoda " incident ", which happened shortly afterwards.

The Fashoda incident is well worth remembering.

## Power, Interests, and Politics

When the British General Kitchener met the French Major Marchand sitting with a handful of French troops across his path southwards in an African village, France and Britain came very near to war. And the war would not have been fought for a mudflat on the river Nile, but as a test of power in a conflict of " major interests ". The question raised was control of Egypt and domination in Africa. To understand Fashoda you have to go back to the year 1892. In that year the French realized that Mr. Gladstone was not going to evacuate Egypt. In 1893 the French Government was encouraged by the report of a certain M. Prompt, an engineer, to think that they could successfully pursue their conflict of interests with Britain in Egypt and the Sudan by the use of power and an ingenious scheme. M. Prompt had reported that by constructing a dam on the lower Sobat river it would be possible to cut off the water supply of Egypt in summer.[1] The British in a waterless Egypt would be forced to negotiate and the conflict of national interests would be resolved in the favour of France. It was with this object that after 1893 the French Government sent first Monteil and then Marchand with a mission to establish a French force on the Nile, and it was an integral part of the plan that this force should be reinforced by an Abyssinian army. The French and Abyssinians

[1] It is amusing to find that M. Prompt was eventually proved to have been completely mistaken.

would then hold Egypt at their mercy and finally wreck the Cape-to-Cairo scheme.[1]

When, therefore, Kitchener found Marchand barring the path of " Britain " to the south, there was no doubt on either side of the Channel that a conflict of major interests had arisen and that the test must be power. Almost the whole of Britain—Conservatives and Liberals and the newspapers of every political colour—were against any kind of negotiation or compromise and were in favour of war if Marchand was not unconditionally withdrawn by the French Government. On October 19th, in a public speech, Sir Michael Hicks-Beach, Chancellor of the Exchequer, announced that " the country has put its foot down. If, unhappily, another view should be taken elsewhere, we, the Ministers of the Queen, know what our duty demands. It would be a great calamity. . . . But there are greater evils than war." On October 28th, Lord Esher wrote to his son that—

> . . . at the Cabinet it was settled that Goschen was to concentrate his fleet and that the French were to be told we could not negotiate until Marchand is out of Fashoda. So that they will have to recall him or fight. It is an anxious moment. Lord Salisbury was the most worried of the Ministers. The others seemed to take the view that the row would have to come, and that it might as well come now as later.

[1] See *The Diplomacy of Imperialism, 1890–1902*, by William L. Langer, vol. II, pp. 558 and ff. This book gives one of the best accounts and analyses of this incident.

And on the same day Lord Esher records in his diary that he went in the evening to an Eton dinner and there he met Lord Rosebery, ex-Liberal Prime Minister. After dinner they walked about the streets of London talking, and somewhere in a London street on October 28th, 1898, this statesman, who had held the office of Foreign Secretary and Prime Minister, told Lord Esher that he was " inclined to think that a war with France now would simplify difficulties in the future ". And the British newspapers were no less blind to the future than the statesman.

> In almost complete unison the British press launched an attack against the French. Here and there a liberal paper like the *Manchester Guardian* kept its head, but many of the British journals were abusive and most of them uncompromising. Marchand's party was described as a band of " irregular marauders " and as the " scum of the desert ". The newspapers were impatient of negotiation and wholly averse to elaborate arguments. In the British view the whole Marchand mission was a demonstration of " indubitable hostility " and of " conscious antagonism " to England. Marchand was an intruder, who would have to be ejected, even though it meant an ultimatum, mobilization and war.[1]

The test of power ended in the favour of Great Britain. There were several reasons for this. The French plan itself miscarried ; it was an integral part of it that Marchand should have the support of the Abyssinians, but the Abyssinian army never

[1] Ibid., p. 552.

arrived and strategically Marchand's position was impossible. In France itself the country was in the throes of the Dreyfus case and the French fleet was in no condition to do battle with the British. The French yielded and Marchand was withdrawn ; the Sudan fell to Britain and power determined the conflict of national interests against France.

Here is an actual case which exactly conforms to the picture of international relations and the part which national interests and power play in them which Professor Carr and those who regard such phenomena as inevitable draw for us.[1] And it was not an exceptional case ; it was characteristic of the international relations between Britain and France (and the other states of Europe) and of the axioms of their policy between 1890 and 1900. The interests of the two states were or were assumed to be in conflict ; what benefited the one harmed the other and vice versa. If the interests were sufficiently " important ", it was for the stronger Power to impose its will upon the weaker, either by war or the threat of war. The realities determining the

---

[1] It is worth while quoting Mr. Langer's summing up : " A mere review of this evidence will show that the Marchand mission was not a ' French picnic party that was outstaying its welcome ', and that the British government could not and did not regard it as such. Here was a question which involved the whole welfare of Egypt. Salisbury was determined not to yield, not to consider any concessions to the French view. *That being the case, it became chiefly a problem of power.* Marchand could easily have been swept aside by the forty thousand troops of Kitchener, but that would have meant a war between England and France. This was realized in London, but the government did not shrink from the prospect." The italics are mine.

relations of the French and British peoples were therefore interests, the conflict of their interests, and their relative power. Cabinet Ministers who were or had been responsible for determining policy took the view that " a row " would have to come with France and that " it might as well come now as later " or that perhaps " a war with France now would simplify difficulties later ".

And then a strange—on this hypothesis regarding the nature of states and international relations, an inexplicable—thing happened. Exactly five years after Fashoda, in the autumn of 1903, the Foreign Secretaries of France and Britain, M. Delcassé, who had originally approved the sending of the Marchand expedition, and Lord Lansdowne, who had been Secretary of State for War in 1898 and was therefore one of the Ministers who thought that the row " might as well come now as later ", sat down together to consider the general question of French and British relations and the particular questions of their conflicting interests. They attempted to do this on an entirely different system from that adopted by them only five years before ; they attempted to regulate the relations of France and Britain, not by conflict and power, but by co-operation, compromise, and agreement. And instead of failing, as they must have done if conflicting interests and power are the " realities " which inevitably determine the relations of sovereign states and the fate of their doomed inhabitants, they completely suc-

171

ceeded. They effected a revolution in Anglo-French policy and relations, and the revolution was determined not by power, realism, or utopianism, but mainly by psychology.

In 1903 the relations between the two countries were completely and permanently changed, not owing to any change in their existing interests or in the relative power of Britain and France, but by a decision of their governments, and this decision was the result of a psychological change. Lansdowne and Delcassé did not suddenly see that the conflicting interests of the two countries had suddenly become " unreal " and the common interests " real ", and there is of course every reason for believing that some important interests of France have been in conflict and others in common with those of Britain (and vice versa) since 1903 just as they were before 1903. But the two statesmen and their governments had come to the common-sense conclusion that in general and in the long run the two countries would gain more by co-operating in common interests and by attempting to compose conflicting interests through compromise than by each of them pursuing its own interest by means of power at the expense of the other. In other words they did exactly what the omnibus passengers did when, instead of fighting, they formed the queue.

As soon as this psychological change took place and the two governments approached one another in a spirit of co-operation instead of conflict, it had a devastating effect upon the importance of " interests " and power as elements in the relation between the two states. All the vital interests, which for the better part of a century had at intervals created danger of war between France and Britain, now proved to be capable of settlement by compromise and co-operation. From 1815 to 1904 the relative power of the two countries had been an element of primary importance in their relations and their policy; from 1904 to 1940 it has been practically negligible. During the last thirty-five years no British Government, in framing its armaments programme, has for one moment considered the relative size of the British and French fleets from the point of view of their being used against each other as instruments of power in a struggle over conflicting interests—any more than the Danish Government frames its armaments policy on the supposition that it may have to use its army against Sweden. But, once more, there is no reason to believe that, by a dispensation of Providence, there are no conflicting interests between Denmark and Sweden or, since 1904, between Britain and France. The explanation of the change since 1904, which has ruled out war as a possibility between Britain and France and has now led people even to propose that the two countries should federate in a single state, is that once the objective of policy had been changed by the Entente, power became a negligible and inappropriate instrument of that policy. This

173

shows the absurdity of ascribing some peculiar and mysterious quality of " reality " to power in international relations. Power is a very real and important element in human society, just as are law, co-operation, stupidity, ideas, beliefs, and ideals ; its importance at any particular moment depends to a very large extent upon the social or political objective which at that moment individuals pursue and the methods by which they choose to pursue it.

There is absolutely no reason to believe that the change which took place in 1904 in the national policies and international relations of France and Britain could not also take place in the policies and international relations of all the Great Powers, or all the states, of Europe. It is no answer to say that it was only fear of Germany which made France and Britain co-operate instead of fighting one another and that their co-operation was directed *against* another Power. To say that is to admit that psychology, and not " reality ", power, and conflict of interests, is the primary determinant in the international situation. If fear of Germany was sufficient to turn France and Britain away from the pursuit of their " real " conflicting interests into the pursuit of their " utopian " harmony of interests and so to eliminate the probability—one might almost say, the possibility—of war between them for half a century, there is no reason, except psychology, why fear of mutual destruction should not effect a similar change in the policies of all European states.

We have now examined the first and the most fundamental argument against the possibility of a League system. The argument does not hold water, because it is made up of metaphor, illusion, emotion, muddled thinking, and vague language. It only appeals to so many people because at bottom it is a rationalization of the emotions of nationalism. But if anything is certain in this doubtful world of 1940 it is that the one way for Europeans to save themselves from self-destruction is to find common-sense means of controlling their national passions instead of bad reasons for making those passions the masters of our destiny.

That is the real international problem which confronts Europe and civilization to-day. It is not a choice between utopia and reality. There is nothing essential or peculiar in the interests and power of sovereign states which made the League utopian and its failure inevitable, or which makes it impossible for human beings to substitute an international system based upon law, compromise, and regulated co-operation for that of conflicting interests, power politics, and war. The choice is between the psychology of conflicting interests and the organization of power politics, on the one hand, and the psychology of common interests and the organization of international co-operation, on the other. The psychology of common interests and of co-operation and peace is there ; it is, no doubt, weak, but it is, none the less, there and has widened and deepened in the last century. Among ordinary persons of all classes, in nearly every state in Europe (including Germany and Italy), in the British Dominions, and over the whole of North America, it is far stronger than it was fifty years ago, though many of them are still unaware that it is incompatible with the doctrines and passions of nationalism and nationalistic imperialism with which they are still infected. Except in the south-east, it is universal in the small European states, and is now so deeply and widely seated in the minds of their populations that it habitually determines their international relations and the foreign policy of all their governments. But even in the great " imperialistic " Powers it is now sufficiently strong to affect the policy of their governments. In all the democratic Great Powers there has been during this century a marked movement away from the imperialism of the nineteenth century, based upon conflict and exploitation, towards a system based upon self-government, compromise, economic planning, and co-operation.[1]

---

[1] The existence and significance of this movement are described and analysed with great acuteness in a recent book, *The Totalitarian Enemy*, by F. Borkenau. Mr. Borkenau points out that " the trend of German imperialism is in direct opposition to the trend of development of the democratic countries. On the whole the imperialistic attitude . . . has considerably declined among democratic nations. The mandate system has made a breach in the old colonial policy. Britain has taken far-reaching measures towards Indian self-government ; the United States have released their hold upon Cuba and upon the Philippines. A large body of

## Power, Interests, and Politics

And it has not been confined to liberals, utopians, Little Englanders, and pacifists. A notable example of it has been the attitude of the " capitalist " and conservative classes in Great Britain towards the claims of the " unsatisfied " Powers which has amazed so many foreign observers during the years since 1925. According to the doctrines of orthodox neo-Marxism and Professor Carr's theory of conflicting interests and power, it was precisely these classes which should have been most forward in opposing the imperialist adventures of Japan, Italy, and Germany. In the Far East, in our African empire, in the Mediterranean and Spain, the most vital economic and strategic interests of Britain were openly menaced. But the old John Bull of the imperialist nineteenth century seemed to have completely died out of the capitalist, governing class in Britain ; it was they who refused a policy of opposition and conflict and promoted that of appeasement, compromise, and co-operation.[1]

And it is not true that, as is often alleged, the

public opinion favours an international redistribution of raw materials. The era of democratic imperialism is over.

" This development is the more interesting because it does not go with a return to free trade. The trend is quite definitely in the direction of international economic planning combined with political and cultural self-government for the smaller nations. It is an emphatically progressive trend ; it is one of the points where the democracies are not lagging behind, but have far outstripped the Fascist Powers. For the latter are now taking up the policy of an exclusive imperialism which the democracies are about to abandon."

[1] See on this point an article by Sir Norman Angell, " The New John Bull ", in the *Political Quarterly* of July–September, 1936.

177

psychology and doctrine of co-operation and common interests as against those of conflict and power are always the assumptions of " a prosperous and privileged class " who are dominant in the community in order " to justify and maintain their dominant position " and resist the claims of the " have-nots ".[1] The slightest study of the habits of animals and of human beings, and of the history of human society, shows that there are two " fundamental types of human behaviour ": one that of conflict or fighting between individuals and groups, the other that of peaceful co-operation.[2] The habit of individual or social co-operation in what appear to be common interests is just as " real " and as widespread as the habit of struggle and fighting for what appear to be conflicting interests. To say that co-operation and the assumption of a common interest, and therefore the exclusion of conflict, are always correlated with the privilege or dominance of an individual or class is sheer nonsense. It implies that in fact there are no such things as common interests. When the omnibus passengers give up fighting for a seat and form a queue, co-operation in the common interest of getting home as quickly as possible takes the place of struggle to be the first person in the omnibus. But

---

[1] The argument is used in its most extreme and absurd form in Professor Carr's book, *The Twenty Years' Crisis*, p. 102 and ff.

[2] See on this point *Personal Aggressiveness and War*, by E. F. M. Durbin and E. J. M. Bowlby, and *The Politics of Democratic Socialism*, Part I, by E. F. M. Durbin.

the co-operation and common interest are not correlated with privilege and dominance. On the contrary, the rule of co-operation here tells against the privilege and dominance of the physically strong. So too in international relations, it is not the Great Powers, satisfied or unsatisfied, who have most persistently in the last fifty years abandoned conflict and power politics for a policy of peaceful co-operation, but the small democratic states of northern Europe.

This is exactly what one would expect to happen. In general, whether among individuals, groups, classes, or nations, it is conflict which produces and maintains privilege and dominance, for it enables those who at the moment have the power to promote what they consider to be their own immediate interests at the expense of everyone else. Regulated co-operation in common interests always entails the control of power, the curtailment or abolition of privilege and dominance, and the establishment of new social " realities ", like law, equality, and justice.

There is, however, a half-truth of great importance in the false view with regard to privilege, dominance, and co-operation which we have just examined. To pass from any social system or organization based upon conflict and the unregulated use of power, to one based upon co-operation, compromise, and law, always presents peculiar difficulties. In history and all human affairs it is never possible to turn over a page and begin writing on an absolutely clean sheet of paper. Every page is blotted with the sins and stupidities of the fathers which are visited upon the children for generation after generation. That is one of the most terrible difficulties with which Europeans are now faced in international relations. A system of conflict and power always establishes a privileged and dominant class. To pass from it to a system of law and peaceful co-operation raises two questions : (1) How are the existing privileges of the dominant class to be dealt with under the new regime ? (2) How are the claims to equality of those who failed to win the prizes under the regime of conflict against those who won the prizes to be dealt with ?

These questions are at the root of the claims of the unsatisfied Powers, Germany, Italy, and Japan. The difficulty is that those claims are " good " only if the nineteenth-century system of conflict and power politics persists, while at the same time under that system they are also " bad " claims. If international relations are to be determined by conflicting interests and the test is to be power and war, then we have no reason to complain against " aggression " by Germany or Italy. On the other hand, if that is to be the international system, Germany and Italy have no reason to complain about " injustice " in the Versailles treaty or in their exclusion from colonial empire. They cannot have it both ways ; if they reject international co-operation, law, and peace, and rely upon power and war and then lose, they cannot then turn round and claim the benefits of the system of co-operation.

But much the same applies, upside down, to those on the other side of the frontiers. While it is not true that law, co-operation, and common interests are always the doctrine and assumptions of the dominant class, it is true that they can be and often are used as the buttresses and protection of privileges and interests consolidated under a system of conflict. The satisfied Powers, if there are any, cannot have it both ways, any more than unsatisfied Powers, if there are any. The demands of Germany, Italy, and Japan have no justification except in a system of conflict and war, and Hitler is the *reductio ad absurdum* or *ad mortem* of that system. He is trying to base international relations solely upon conflicting interests and power, and this, if it persists in the modern world, means either the anarchical dissolution of Europe or the establishment of a slave empire. The only alternative is that Europe should order its international relations on a system of law, co-operation, and peace. That, however, is not possible, unless the system applies to all and unless no state continues to enjoy the advantages and privileges which it previously gained under the system of conflicting interests and war. In other words, both the methods which we have seen employed in other directions to solve the social problem of conflicting interests must be adapted to international relations. There will always remain certain conflicting interests between states, but there is, as we have seen, no reason why they should be settled by power and war. They must be settled by law, compromise, and regulated co-operation. But it is also possible and necessary to alter some of the conditions which create the conflict of interests, and the most important factor here is the power politics system itself. For instance, the exclusive colonial imperialist empire is the creation of the power politics system, and the economic advantages of a colonial empire are an important result of it. But once an exclusive empire has come into existence, it is itself the cause of a new conflict of interests, if it is used by the imperialist Power *against* the rest of the world. Its existence is consistent with a system of conflict and war, but is inconsistent with a system of co-operation and peace. Imperialist Powers, like France and Britain, cannot, therefore, have it both ways. Here it is essential that they should alter the conditions which create the conflict of interests. If they want an international system of peaceful co-operation, they must divest themselves of all the economic advantages and privileges of empire which they won under the system of power and war.

But in the last paragraph we have already passed from the subject which we were discussing, namely whether a League system of international co-operation is impossible, to a completely different subject, namely how such a system can be established and what are the conditions necessary for its functioning. We have in fact passed naturally to the questions which must be dealt with in the chapter which follows. For we have found that there is nothing in the nature of the sovereign state, its interests and power, which makes utopian or impossible an international system of co-operation and peace, in which law is established and power controlled. We now have to examine the other objections against the League system established in 1919. Those who make them do not say that a pacific international system is impossible, but that the League system contained certain fundamental defects which made its failure inevitable. If we are to learn from the experience of the war of 1914, and if we are to attempt at the end of the present war to prevent a third, it is essential to consider those objections carefully, so that we may get into our heads now some idea of what the international system must be if Europe is to escape the perpetual menace of totalitarian warfare. That is the subject of the next chapter.

CHAPTER III

PEACE

THE objections to the League system, as established in 1919, which we now have to examine, were stated briefly on pages 107–9. I propose to consider them in the light of the following political postulates or axioms. These postulates will, of course, be rejected by those who take the " realist " view which was dealt with in the previous chapter and who maintain that international relations *must* inevitably be based upon conflict and power. But they are, I believe, implicit in the facts, given in the last chapter, which refute the " realist " view and they will, therefore, be accepted by all those who hold that there is nothing peculiar in that type of human organization known as the sovereign state which makes it impossible to subject its power to international control and to organize its relations with other states on a basis of law, compromise, and cooperation. The postulates are these. The problem of inter-state relations which has become so acute in the nineteenth and twentieth centuries is a problem of communal government which does not differ essentially from hundreds of other similar problems which have confronted human beings during the last 3,000 years. As was pointed out in the first chapter, we have so long an experience of government in human society that we already know what conditions, in broad outline, must be fulfilled if the problem is to be solved, i.e. if the relations between these organized groups of individuals, called states, are to be determined peacefully by co-operation instead of by conflict and power. In the first place, there must be a regular, agreed method and organization for resolving conflicts of interest by compromise and co-operation or of altering particular conditions which create a conflict of interest. Secondly, there must be a regular, agreed method and organization for impartial third-party decisions in case of disputes between states. Thirdly, there must be a regular agreed method and organization for making the general laws which are to govern the relations of states and for making general changes in their relations required by changed conditions. Fourthly, there must be some agreement with regard to the control or non-control of national power, and in particular as to the action of the community of states should one of its members, in breach of its obligations, resort to aggression, conflict, or war.

If the reader will turn to page 100, he will see that the constitution of the League and the obligations assumed by its members, which are summarized there, were an attempt to fulfil these four conditions precedent to peace. Once it is admitted that *an* international system for preventing war is not utopian because of the nature of the sovereign state, the question whether *the* League system or any other proposed system is workable depends upon three factors. It will work only if (1) its principles and objects, and the form of its organization, conform to the psychology, the beliefs and desires, of those who will have to work it ; (2) if it makes adequate provision for dealing with the interests and power of states and peoples ; (3) if the machinery of its organization is really adapted to the functions which it will have to perform.[1] The general criticisms of the League system which we shall now have to examine will be found in each case to turn upon one or more of these three factors.

Let us begin by considering the objection to the League which is numbered (2) on page 107. Those who make this objection maintain that the League failed as an international system of co-operation because it did not go far enough, because it was an alliance or confederation of sovereign states and not a federation in which the separate states merged their sovereignty. Only a federation, it is alleged, can create a permanent and stable system of inter-

---

[1] This is only a particular instance of the general truth that the most important factors which determine politics and society are three, and that they always act and react upon one another : (1) Beliefs and desires, i.e. psychology ; (2) Interests, and (3) Power. I have dealt with this truth more fully in my other books, i.e. *After the Deluge*, vols. I and II, and *Barbarians at the Gate*, particularly pp. 100–140.

national co-operation which will prevent conflict
and war, for if states retain their independence and
sovereignty, common action in a crisis where there
is a conflict of interests will sooner or later prove
impossible and the alliance or confederation will
break up. The actual history of the League's
failure proves this.

This view raises a fundamental question with
regard to the League and any future attempt to
prevent war. Whether the federal or the League
system is preferable will depend upon their relation
to two of the three factors mentioned above, the
existing social psychology of the European and the
adaptability of the two systems of organization to
the functions which we wish them to perform.
Formally the difference between a federation and
an alliance or confederation is a difference of
political organization and machinery. And the
difference is mainly confined to that part of the
organization which makes the general laws governing the relations of the groups, which makes changes
in those relations when they are demanded by
changed conditions, and which controls the power
of the several groups and of the whole organization.
The difference between a confederation of states to
prevent war and a federation to prevent war would,
therefore, be found in those organs of government
which in the League system were called the Council
and the Assembly ; the other organs, e.g. the international court, might well be exactly the same

under both systems. Under the League or any other confederate system each state enters and remains in the confederation as an independent unit, and in the organs which make the general laws or fundamental changes in international society it is represented by its government. In a federation each state enters as an independent unit, but, when it has entered, it is merged for certain specific purposes in a new unit of government or state. The Council or the Assembly or both would be a federal body, and states would be represented in the federal organ, not by their governments, but by representatives specially elected or chosen. The several states are therefore merged for federal purposes in a new super-state which must itself have a federal executive government. The powers of the federal government and of the states governments have to be defined, and once the federation has been formed, the government of a state has no say with regard to any subject or powers which have been handed over to the federation and its federal organ.

Which of these two systems is most likely, in the present state of Europe, to establish an international system based upon law, compromise, and co-operation instead of conflict and war will depend, as was said above, upon the efficiency of each organization to perform its functions and the relation of each to the existing social psychology of Europeans. Let us deal first with the efficiency of the two types of organization, considered merely as social machinery. Theoretically and ideally the federal type of organization has great advantages over the other as a method of regulating the relations of groups by law and agreement, settling or eliminating conflicts of interest, and controlling the power of groups in the interests of the community. One of the chief reasons for the international crises which have continually increased in number and in intensity during the last hundred years, and for the international anarchy of power politics and totalitarian war which threatens to destroy us all, is that the economic and political, the whole social development, of the world during that period demanded economic, political, and social planning on an international scale, i.e. international government, and that the psychology of nationalism has persistently prevented or sterilized the growth of international government. The kind of society which has developed in, say, Germany and Britain since 1800—and that means, though people who write books are apt to forget it, the kind of life which individuals living in Berlin or London, in Pomerania or Sussex, actually live—is the result of changes in the economic and social systems and in individual and social psychology. Those changes and the results of them are facts ; they exist here to-day in Europe before our eyes, and no one, not even a dictator, though he may ignore them or deny them, can prevent their existence or the effects of their existence. One effect of their existence is that the social and economic system of Germany and Britain creates an intricate system of economic and social relations between the inhabitants of those two countries and between each of them and the rest of the world. To imagine that relations of such number and intricacy can be left to regulate themselves without any international organization or government is a delusion which could be held only by a fervent patriot, a realist, or a dictator.

Europeans are faced with one of those social dilemmas which are so frequent in the human race. They desire two things which are socially incompatible. They can have the highly industrialized society which has actually developed with its closely articulated economic and social relations spreading out from all the centres of population, like the veins and arteries of communal life, throughout the world, and in that case it is absolutely essential that international should supersede national government in many spheres of that life. Or they can have the isolated, autarkic, narrowly and passionately national state, rejecting all kinds of international government or control, organized to pursue its own " interests " *against* the rest of the world. They can have the one or the other, but they cannot have both. For the autarkic, isolated national state is an antediluvian anachronism from the pre-industrial age ; it is incompatible with the society which was already in existence in 1914. Ever since the end of the last war, we have been watching in the crisis of European civilization the effect of human beings trying at one and the same time to establish these two mutually incompatible and contradictory forms of society. The plain truth is that the logic of facts is forcing us to choose between these two incompatibles ; we can go forward to the next stage of industrialized civilization with international government, or we can reject international government, in which case we shall have to retreat into the pre-industrialized age.

If one looks at the federal system merely from the point of view of social machinery, it is certainly, in theory, the most suitable for international government. It has already been tried with success, in the United States for instance, where the problem arose of establishing the relations of large and distinct groups on a basis of law and co-operation instead of conflict and where it was desirable to unite the groups under a common government for some purposes while keeping them separate under separate governments for other purposes. That, of course, is essentially the same problem which confronts Europeans to-day. We want to establish the relations of European states on a basis of law and co-operation instead of conflict, power, and war, and to unite them for certain purposes under international government, while, at the same time, leaving them for other purposes to control their own affairs. Federal union would unite what are now sovereign, independent states in a new federal state with a new federal government which would control all those departments of national life over which it was given jurisdiction. Presumably as a minimum, it would have jurisdiction over what are now inter-state relations, including economic relations, and foreign policy, and over armaments and armed forces. In all such matters the individual states would cease to be sovereign. Britain or France, for instance, would no longer have a Foreign Minister and the British or French parliament would no longer have any control over foreign policy ; the decision would rest with the Federal Assembly, Cabinet, and Foreign Minister. Similarly the governments of France and Britain would have no control over their tariff and currency policies or, probably, over such questions as immigration and emigration ; these questions would be decided by the Federal government. National currencies and national armies, navies, and air-forces would cease to exist ; they would be federal and under federal control.

It is obvious that a system of this kind, viewed merely as the machinery of government, is much more closely articulated than a confederation of states which, as in the League, are bound together for specific purposes by specific obligations. A federation cuts the Gordian knot and directly sub-stitutes international for national government. If it could be effectively established it would therefore have great advantages over the League system. It provides the social machinery for international planning, for resolving conflicts of interest by compromise and co-operation, for altering the conditions which create existing conflicts, for making the rules and laws which are essential in international society, and for regulating, controlling, or eliminating the use of power by those groups of individuals which we now call sovereign, independent states. Some form of international federation is, in fact, the kind of organization which an industrialized society such as that in which we live clearly demands. We may destroy civilization as it developed in the last century and go back to a less closely articulated form of society, calling old barbarisms by new names, and in that case we may do without any closely articulated social organization and machinery of government ; but if nineteenth-century civilization is to go on developing to a further stage, then federation in some form or other is inevitable.

But, as we have frequently had to point out, in the problem of war or peace which we are considering in this book there are two factors of great importance which act and react upon each other, the organization and machinery of international society and psychology. We now have to examine the relation between the communal psychology of Europeans and these two forms of international organization, federation and a confederation like the League. Communal psychology played a very large part in causing the failure of the League.

There are, as we have seen, two opposite or contradictory trends of international communal psychology in the Europeans of to-day. Both exist
and both are " real ". The future of Europe
depends upon which of them gains ascendancy and
so determines the pattern of international relations.
It is at this point that the importance of the interaction between the psychology and organization
of government comes in. The two trends may be
conveniently labelled the psychology of nationalism and the psychology of internationalism. The
nationalist psychology is the psychology of exclusive
national interests ; it regards the interests of one's
own country as peculiarly sacred and those of other
countries as either inimical or no concern of oneself.
It regards conflict between states as " natural " and
the use of power to determine their relations as
" inevitable ". The nationalist, who, when any
political question has to be considered within the
ring fence of his own frontiers, instinctively considers
it in terms of law, compromise, agreement, or co-
operation, instinctively considers any international
question in terms of conflict and power. This
psychology is manured emotionally by patriotism,
fear, and hatred, and where circumstances encourage
those emotions, it flourishes in devastating luxuri-
ance. The psychology of internationalism is the
opposite of this ; it is the psychology of co-operation,
compromise, law, and agreement. We have seen
it at work in the smaller states of northern Europe,

in the revolt of the common people against the results of the policy and psychology of conflict, power, and war, and in the diplomatists and governments of France and Britain since 1904.

If Europe is to pass from an international system of conflict and war to one of law and co-operation, the machinery of its organization must be such as encourages the growth of the psychology of internationalism at the expense of the psychology of nationalism. This is an extremely important and delicate practical question, such as frequently occurs in the political and other problems of life. You have to be bold and cautious at the same time. You have to provide the means by which the psychology of international law and co-operation may become more and more effective, and yet at the same time you must make due allowance for the opposite psychology of nationalism and conflict. You must go far enough to break with the past and its vicious circle, but you must not go too far, or the psychology which creates the vicious circle will destroy you, your organization, and itself.

The history of the League teaches us a lesson in this respect. The failure of the League was not due to only one cause—historical events of that kind are never due to a single cause. But there can be no doubt that the communal psychology of nationalism played a very large part in causing its failure. And I do not mean by that the obvious and crude fact that it was destroyed by the psychology of

nationalism, power politics, and aggression in the
fascist states who were openly out to destroy the
League and its system of peaceful co-operation. I
mean that it was destroyed by the nationalism of
those peoples and governments who were attempting
to establish a system of peace and law. No international system which is intended to substitute law
and co-operation for power politics and war will
work unless those who " work " it have the psychology of law and co-operation. That means that
they must feel and believe that the establishment
and preservation of the rule of law, the peaceful
settlement of disputes, the prevention of war, and
resistance to aggression are national interests and
of vital concern to themselves and to their country.
They must be prepared to make the sacrifices which
law, justice, equity, and peace inevitably demand
from individuals and communities.

The failure of the League was not entirely, but
very largely, due to the fact that this psychology
was non-existent or was weak in those who sincerely
desired law and peace and even in many of those
who were sincere in their belief that the League
system was almost the only hope of obtaining them.
The cause of this failure in psychology was mainly
the persistence and strength of the psychology of
nationalism ; the effect was to make the supporters
of law and peace unwilling to run the risks or make
the sacrifices which law and peace inevitably require
from their worshippers. Take, first, the case of

## Peace

Mr. Chamberlain, Sir John Simon, Mr. Baldwin, and the whole National Government from the time of the Manchurian aggression of Japan to the final aggression of Germany upon Poland. They were sincere in their desire for the maintenance of law and the preservation of peace ; Mr. Baldwin and Mr. Chamberlain, in so far as they are capable of human passion, were passionate for peace. But until the threat to Poland, their attitude was that of Cain when the voice of the Lord was heard saying : " Where is Abel (or China or Abyssinia or Spain or Czechoslovakia) thy brother ? " ; their answer was : " I know not : Am I my brother's keeper ? " or even : " Czechoslovakia is far away and small and I know very little about it ; I am not its brother and not its keeper." The answer was inconsistent with the obligations of these statesmen and their government under the Covenant of the League ; it was inconsistent with the system of collective security to which they were bound, but which they then believed to be utopian.[1] But— what is more important—it was inconsistent with any kind of international system based upon law and peace, for it implied that the preservation of law and peace was not itself a national interest and that national interests are the old, narrow, exclusive interests of every nation for itself and the devil or

---

[1] This raises, of course, the whole question of sanctions, which will have to be considered below in its relation to a peace system like the League.

the stronger take the weaker. Those who still maintain that collective security, i.e. collective resistance to aggression, is a wrong or utopian system for establishing international law and peace can still legitimately maintain that these statesmen were right. But the statesmen themselves cannot do so, for by their guarantee to Poland and Rumania and by their declaration of war upon Germany, they have confessed that they were wrong and have adopted themselves—perhaps too late—the system and psychology of internationalism which they had previously denied.

But the failure in psychology was not confined to the Right and those who disliked the whole idea of the League ; it can also be observed among many on the Left and among that vast mass of people who belonged permanently neither to Right nor Left, but looked to the League to answer their only articulate political cry : " Never again ". The Labour Party, for instance, always officially stood for the League system and for Britain fulfilling her obligations under the Covenant. But there was this weakness in the Party's position, that while it urged resistance to aggression as the only possi- bility of establishing law and peace, when it came to the question of providing the armaments which resistance would have required, it hesitated. Its hesitation was, no doubt, partly due to a not un- reasonable mistrust of the National Government and the European policy of the Prime Minister, but

it was also due to a failure among many of its supporters to understand the demands of a peace
system or to meet those demands if they did understand them. This was still more true of the vast
numbers of people of no particular permanent
political allegiance, referred to above, who had
voted in the Peace Ballot for the full implication
of the League system. The view, popular now
because of the sequel, that the voters were merely
ignorant and deluded people and their vote of no
real significance is short-sighted. These people
had a truer sense of the realities in the international
situation than most of the statesmen who were then
conducting our affairs. But the sense was too dim
and uninstructed to counteract the psychology of
nationalism in which we have all grown up and
which takes the narrow view of national interests
and therefore of the interests which the nation
should defend. They were not then prepared, as
they are to-day—*mirabile dictu*—under the leadership of Mr. Neville Chamberlain, to treat law and
peace everywhere in Europe as one of the greatest
of national interests and to fulfil the demands of
a peace system by resisting aggression whether it
is against Poland or Norway, Rumania or Finland.

It is important to emphasize the difference between
the view of national interests and their effects taken
in the preceding paragraphs and the view which
was criticized earlier. The " realists " maintain
that there is something inherent in national interests

which makes them objectively conflicting and that, therefore, it is a delusion to think that, for instance, there can be any common interest among all nations in peace. It is a theory which has been developed in order to rationalize the emotions of nationalism, and international conflict, and it is perpetually used by statesmen, consciously or unconsciously, when they wish to justify the use of force, conflict, conquest, or refusal to co-operate. The whole argument of this book is that the theory is false and based upon a superficial view of the nature of social " interests ". There is no such thing as an objective social " interest " ; the interests of any social group, such as a class or nation, at any particular moment are not determined solely by objective facts, but by the interaction of objective facts, social organization, and psychology, i.e. by the beliefs of the individuals in the class or nation as to what is or is not to their interest. " Realists " deride the view that there can be a harmony of interest among all nations in peace. But the whole history of Europe since 1815 makes it probable that the view is correct. It is true that at any particular moment, if the international system is based upon conflict and the psychology of the majority of Europeans is nationalist, it may be to the immediate interest of a particular nation not to keep the peace. But for the realist to say that would be to beg the question. For by changing the system and psychology the interest of that nation might have been served far better by peace than war. That people, looking round Europe to-day, can refuse to change the word " might " in the last sentence into " would " reduces one to amazed despair. If facts be the test of truth and of theories, then the plain truth is that in the long run there is not one single nation in Europe which has gained anything by any war in the last hundred years, that in the long run no class in any nation has gained anything by any war, and that not 5 per cent of the individuals in any class in any nation have gained anything by any war. That means that all the nations, all the classes in the nations, and ˙95 per cent of the individuals in the classes would to-day be better off and have gained more, both spiritually and materially, if there had been no wars during the last hundred years. If that does not mean that all nations have a common interest in peace and in preventing war, then human life, history, and politics are all meaningless.

But though the objective view of interests is false, . the psychological view of interests is unfortunately true. The League failed because the psychology of co-operation was weak or absent. What holds national life together and makes the machinery of national government and society work is a sense of the common interest in law, co-operation, and peace ; it is impossible to hold international society together and make machinery of international government work unless there is a sense of the common international interest in law, co-operation, and peace. That sense is, as I have said, to-day weak or absent, and that fact destroyed the League. There is no reason either in history or facts why that sense should not be developed in the near future sufficiently to prevent totalitarian war and the destruction of Europe. But the difficulty must not be ignored and we must learn our lesson from the experience of the League.

One lesson is that the machinery of international organization must adapt itself to existing psychology. It must provide for the development from nationalist to international psychology, from the psychology of conflict to the psychology of co-operation and law. But it must not be too far ahead of the existing nationalist psychology, because, if it is, instead of encouraging, it will prevent that development. Leaving aside for the moment the question whether the League type of organization is workable, it may be stated with some confidence that the League, as established in 1919, did not comply with the exigencies of communal psychology. It was established as a world organization for peace and in all circumstances and in every case of international difficulty or dispute there was no differentiation between the obligations imposed upon the states members. When for instance a crisis arose in Europe which obviously vitally affected the interests of half a dozen European states and—perhaps less obviously—all European states, the League system assumed that the interests of any small South-American republic was affected in the same way and imposed upon it the same obligations, though to the ordinary man the crisis seemed to be no concern to anyone in South America. It is arguable and probably true that, if the crisis led to war, it would vitally affect the interests of every state and individual in South America, and that they therefore have a common interest in the settlement of the crisis and the prevention of war. But in the existing state of nationalist and international psychology that view is not taken and there is no possibility of its being taken. When therefore the machinery of international organization imposes obligations or requires action which assume this sense of community and common interest, it fails because the psychology necessary for working it is not and cannot at present exist.

The fact that the League was a world organization, completely undifferentiated, assuming the psychology of a world community in all nations and imposing upon all the same obligations in all cases and in all regions of the world, continually hampered the League and actually prevented the development of the psychology of unity and co-operation essential for its success. This was evident in the great crises of Manchuria and Abyssinia. But to those who took part in or followed the day-to-day and less sensational operations of its Council and Assembly, it was just as evident in them and it led to such proposals as Briand's for "regionalizing" the League.

I shall have to return to this question, but at the moment I am concerned with the lesson which the federalist must learn from this experience. Federation assumes and requires a much greater uniformity of communal organization and of "international" psychology than a confederate system like that of the League. It is, for instance, inconceivable that a dictatorship could be married successfully with a democracy in a federation ; the marriage service might be read over them in a conference and treaty, just as you might read the marriage service over a dog and a cat, but in neither case would the union be real, permanent, or fertile. This is partly because the organization of a dictatorship and democracy would not fit together into the organization and machinery of federation, but also partly because the common social psychology essential for the working of the federal machinery would not be there. A federation of states for the preservation of peace and the prevention of war requires the psychology of co-operation and law in each of the federated states ; democracy itself requires the same psychology if it is to function, but dictatorship is based upon exactly the opposite type of psychology, the psychology of conflict and power. It is a delusion to think that you could produce such political monstrosities as a federation of the Persia of Xerxes with the Athens of Themistocles or of the Spain of General Franco with the democracy of Switzerland and make them live. They would merely remain specimens in the museum of history.

But the difficulty applies not merely to states which have a different political or social system, because one is a dictatorship and the other a democracy. History demonstrates the fact that it is not possible to maintain two communities within a state unless there is an active sense of community, the consciousness of a common objective. It is possible that such a sense and consciousness have developed sufficiently in France and Britain, for instance, to make a federation of the two states for the purposes of peace workable. But the experience of the League gives one no reason for hoping that merely by federating the states of, say, South America with those of Europe you would create the necessary consciousness of community and of the common interest in the preservation of peace. Federation is not a panacea for conflict, as the American Civil War proved. It is only one of several methods of organizing communities on a basis of law and co-operation and of controlling power ; whether in any particular case it is the best will depend upon several factors, one of which is, psychological.

It follows that no world organization of states could possibly function in the world as we now know it, if it were given a federal form. Federal union of sovereign states, if it is used after the war, in the organization of peace, must be on a much more modest scale. Federations of a small number of states, geographically near to one another, belonging to the same stage of civilization, if their political and economic organization is similar or complementary and if psychologically their inhabitants have a sense of unity and common interests, are alone possible. France and Britain, for instance, have in the last thirty years developed a unity of political purpose which makes federation for specific purposes already practical politics. When the present war ends, the reaction against the international system which caused it and belated learning by experience from the Versailles peace may create conditions in which, with France and Britain as a nucleus, a still wider federation of western democracies in Europe, including a democratic Germany, might become possible. At the other end of Europe, along the banks of the Danube, it has for long been recognized by many people that some kind of federation is inevitable, if peace and prosperity are to take the place of the political and economic anarchy which has been the direct result of the power politics of the Balkan sovereign states. Nowhere else in the world is the closest political and economic co-operation between the various states—and therefore some form of federation—more necessary, and nowhere else has the crazy psychology of nationalism and conflict made the common-sense path to peace more difficult. It is said that even the amœba learns by experience ; perhaps after the war of 1939 the Balkan peoples may at last follow the example of the amœba.

In the first flush of the discovery of federation as the panacea of all international and national diseases by Mr. Streit and others, many people went far beyond this kind of programme and talked in terms of world federation. Sensible and sober advocates of federal union now confine themselves to the advocacy of much more modest programmes of the kind suggested above.[1] But while a Peace Federation, limited to some of the west European democracies is a possibility and might, if successfully established, prove a more effective instrument than the League in substituting law and co-operation for power and conflict in Europe, the tremendous forces which stand in its way and which draw their strength from the events of the last twenty years and from contemporary nationalist psychology must not be underestimated. It is necessary to consider them briefly.

In the first place, while a federation between France and Britain alone may be desirable for other reasons, it would not in itself necessarily be a nucleus

[1] Sir William Beveridge, for instance, in his pamphlet *Peace by Federation ?*, published by the Federal Union, proposes a Peace Federation restricted to the following states : Britain, France, Germany, Denmark, Norway, Sweden, Finland, Belgium, Holland, Eire, and the four self-governing Dominions of the British Commonwealth outside Europe. In my opinion this is the extreme limit which would have any chance of success and is probably too ambitious.

of a peace system based upon law and co-operation. On the contrary, if France and Britain were federated and the rest of Europe unorganized in a peace system, the Anglo-French federation would sooner or later become again an alliance of the old type in a system of power politics and conflict. If it were strong enough, it might impose peace upon Europe, and it is possible that an imposed peace of this kind may at the end of the war be the least bad of all the alternatives which face us. But in that case we must not delude ourselves into believing that the lesser evil is a blessing. History proves that there is no permanence in an alliance, a federation, or an international system which depends upon a pre-ponderance of power, if the society is based upon conflict and not law. And the reason is, as we have seen before, that of all the factors which determine the lives of individuals and the history of communities the most unstable is power, except as the sanction of law. A peace imposed by a federation would sooner or later have exactly the same fate as the peace imposed by the alliance at Versailles.

Therefore no federation which did not include a good many of the western democracies, besides France and Britain, could form the basis of a real international system of law and co-operation. Unless Germany were democratized and were a member of the federation, I do not believe that any of the smaller states would agree to enter it. They would regard it, not as the beginning of a peace system, but as an alliance to impose peace upon Germany. The political sins of one generation are visited upon many generations which succeed it. China, Abyssinia, and most fatally Czechoslovakia, are a series of albatrosses which the British Government hung around its own neck and the necks of the League, of Europe, and of peace itself. *The Ancient Mariner* is a true and terrible parable of history and politics. Only when it can be said that

> The man hath penance done,
> And penance more will do,

only when once more " the dead men "—China, Abyssinia, and Czechoslovakia—stand " all together on the deck ", will the " spell " be " snapt " and the albatross fall from our neck. But the small states will never again stand together on the deck, until the Great Powers have convinced them, by really doing penance, that they really intend this time to establish a " peace system ". The blessed word federation will not by itself convince them.

They will only be convinced by a peace the terms of which are themselves a guarantee that the Great Powers of western Europe are determined to substitute law and co-operation for power and conflict as the basis of their political relations. That means that nearly all the fundamental relations and obligations which the League Covenant established in theory, but which were ignored or broken in practice, will have to be made realities. But that will not be enough. No peace system will function if the old system of bitter economic conflict between nations continues. If there is to be peace after this war and any return to prosperity in Europe, international economic planning on a large scale will be necessary, and that means that international economic co-operation, instead of conflict, must be made a reality.

If these conditions are fulfilled and if the war ends with the democratization of Germany, it is just possible that a federation of the scope envisaged by Sir William Beveridge might be established. But it is essential to realize that, even so, under the most favourable conditions, the psychological obstacles are immense. In a federation, even if it be strictly limited to the purposes of peace, the control of foreign relations, as we now know them, including questions of defence and war and peace and almost inevitably economic policy, would be subject to federal government, i.e. to international government in the fullest sense. The governments of France, Britain, and Germany, under the conditions envisaged by Sir William Beveridge, would have no say in these matters. And if inter-state economic relations were controlled by the federal government, that would necessarily impose narrow limits upon the power of each state to determine the nature of its economic, and therefore of its social, system. I am not arguing here that this would be either a good or a bad thing or that the sacrifices of " independence " in all these matters would not be repaid a hundredfold if they won for Europe a century of peace. But they imply a colossal leap forward both from the organization and the psychology of the national state as they exist to-day. The leap is much greater and more difficult than that which the League system demanded, and the League failed because Europeans refused to take the first psychological steps from national conflict to international co-operation which were essential if they wanted peace. It is ominous, too, that in the British Empire, where psychological and other conditions have been far more favourable than in the international sphere, the peoples of the Dominions have consistently refused to enter a federal form of government.

This brings us to an important question with regard to the future international organization for peace. The considerations given above are not intended to show, nor do they show, that a limited use of the federal system is utopian, but they do prove that it will be more difficult to get it accepted and worked than it was even in the case of the League system. And the enthusiasm of federal enthusiasts should not mislead people to believe that federation is the only alternative to the anarchy of national power politics and war. There is nothing in the history of the League's failure which proves that a confederation of states for peace, in which the sovereignty of each is in fact limited by agreement for the purposes of peace, is inherently impossible.

It is never profitable to spend much time over the " ifs " and " ands " and the " might have beens " of history, but at the same time the causes of historical events are so many and so complicated that dogmatic assertion that this or that was inevitable is rarely justified. There was a moment in the history of the League, after the admission of Germany, when, if the tide of world economics—which was entirely unconnected with the League's structure—had begun to flow in a different direction, the League system might have " worked " for another five or ten years without being subjected to the most exacting tests in the most unfavourable conditions, and there is no reason why it should not then have consolidated itself and developed into a real system of law and co-operation. The history of the British Empire during the last sixty years points in the same direction. It is a confederation of states of the same type as the League and it has persistently rejected federation. Its break up has been continually prophesied by realists and theorists, yet it has, on the whole, proved to be no less successful in practice as a system of international relations based upon regulated and pacific co-operation than many federations, and during that period it has stood up to the most terrible test of two totalitarian wars.

The moral is that people in this country would be ill-advised to pin their hope exclusively on federation as the only possible peace system. If federation at the end of the war proves to be impossible, or possible only on an extremely limited scale, the less articulated system of confederation will have to be tried again, if we are not to resign ourselves to permanent anarchy and recurring totalitarian wars. But that leads us to a further point. It has been argued above that the world is not yet psychologically or socially ready for world federation. Federal unions will, therefore, at the best be small and limited. It is conceivable that in Europe we might see a federation for peace of some of the western and northern democracies, or two federations, one of the western democracies and the other of the Scandinavian countries. A Danubian or Balkan federation might also be practical politics. But even if these federations were successfully established, the question of their relation to one another and to the rest of the world remains.

The establishment of limited federations, while it might temporarily reduce the risk of war in certain geographical areas, would not solve the problem which is the subject of this book. The relations of states are not limited geographically, nor will the relations of federated states be limited geographically. International relations are to-day world relations, multifarious and of immense complication. They cannot be carried on without some system of world organization and government. And if the organization is based upon power and conflict, sooner or later totalitarian war will result. It follows that if we do not want totalitarian war, we must develop a world system of interstate relations based upon law and co-operation, and therefore that, if limited federations are successfully established, they must be part of or units in this greater system.

What form can this world system be given, if we are to take into consideration psychological and social conditions in the existing world ? Federation we have seen to be impossible because it is too closely articulated and requires a much greater psychological and social unity than exists at present. The only possible alternative is the looser organization of a confederation, a union, not of peoples within a single state, but of states bound by specific agreements regarding the use of national power, the rule of law, and the practice of co-operation. That means that for world relations we have got once more to try to create a system resembling that of the League.

Here we can learn much from the experience of the League. We remarked above that one of the causes of the League's failure was to be found in its own organization. It imposed certain obligations which assumed an international psychology which does not, and, as things are to-day, cannot be expected to exist. The obligations were connected with the use of power or sanctions, as they are commonly called. In case of breach of the fundamental obligations of the peace system, of aggressive war or the threat of aggression, the Covenant imposed upon all members of the League, irrespective of their geographical or international position, the same obligations to resist aggression. That assumes a sense of world solidarity, of a common interest in peace which does not exist and will not exist at the end of this war.

In the League, and in any international peace system based upon law and co-operation, there are two distinct series of obligations which are vital to the system. The first series creates the method and organization for determining the rules or laws, for dealing with conflicts of interest, and for regulating relations on a basis of compromise and co-operation ; in the analysis of the League system given on pages 100 and 101 this series is represented by the obligations or provisions numbered (1), (3), (5), (6), and (7). The second series deals with the use and control of power or force and is covered on page 100 by the obligations numbered (2) and (4).

This brings us face to face with the third of the four most important causes which, critics of the League maintain, must inevitably bring about the failure of such a system.[1] It is true that the League broke down when the moment came for putting into operation the obligations relating to power and for common action to resist aggression. The League attempted to do for international government what in fact all through history has been done for all other kinds of government based upon law, compromise, and co-operation, i.e. to organize communal power

[1] See p. 107.

as a sanction behind the law. That means that if any member of the community resorts to force, i.e. uses his power to enforce his own interests or to compel other members of the community to do his will in breach of the fundamental laws, the force or power of the whole community is used against him in order to defeat his object. Applied to the relations of states this system would mean that a state making war upon another would be resisted by all the other members of the community of states.

There are two objections to such a system, as we said on page 108. One of these is that of the extreme pacifists who maintain that a system of sanctions for international law and of international collective security, like that of the League, attempts to prevent war by war and to eliminate force by the use of force, and is morally wrong and bound to fail. Emotionally I have the greatest sympathy with the pacifist view. The use of force is always bad in society, and civilization consists largely in the elimination of power and force from human relations and their regulation by other means, e.g. agreed rule, compromise, and co-operation in common ends. If you are on the side of civilization, you must be against the use of force. But that unfortunately does not settle the matter. In human affairs the choice is rarely between what is good and what is bad ; it is usually between what is bad and what is worse. That is pre-eminently the case with the position and control of power and force in human society. The question is whether the unregulated use of power by individuals in their own interest is better or worse than the use of power by a community as the sanction of laws the object of which is to prevent the use of power by individuals in their own interest. The answer of history to this question seems to me unavoidable, namely that in the vast majority of cases the unregulated use of power by individuals is infinitely worse than the communal use of power as the sanction of law, and further that the establishment of a regime of law and non-violence, of co-operation in place of conflict, is rarely, if ever, possible unless the power of the community is used, in the last resort, to maintain the law against those who resort to violence. I see no reason why this rule should not apply to international relations and the society of states ; on the contrary, there is every reason for believing that it does, because the more anarchic the rule of violence, the more essential it is, if we are to decrease the sum of human misery, to establish some communal control of violence.

The pacifist replies that pacifism or non-resistance is not tried, and that, if it were, it would succeed. There is not the slightest evidence for believing that unilateral pacifism would be successful in the actual world of the twentieth century. When I hear the pacifist arguing in this way, I am often reminded of something which I once saw in a Ceylon jungle. It was a pitilessly hot day, in which not a leaf stirred and the sun blazing in a cloudless sky seemed to impose a leaden silence upon the parched earth. I was travelling on foot in thick jungle by narrow game-tracks in uninhabited country. Suddenly I saw upon a tree rather higher than the rest a group of monkeys. Their behaviour was so strange that I stopped behind a large thorn bush to watch them. They jumped up and down, up and down, up and down, always in the same place, raising their thin arms to heaven. And then on the other side of the thorn bush I heard a strange noise—click, click, click. The tracker behind me whispered : " leopard." Then I knew that I was witnessing an incident of jungle life which I had been told of, but had never seen before. When a leopard sees monkeys on a tall tree, he lies down under it and clicks his teeth together. The monkeys, fascinated or hypnotized by the sound, begin to leap up and down, up and down on the branches of the tree above his head. The click, click of the teeth goes on below, and the monkeys leap up and down with their arms raised to heaven above him until sooner or later one of them misses his footing and falls to the ground. He is eaten by the leopard. All my sympathies were, and are, with my collateral ancestor, the grey monkey, the pacifist, silhouetted against the sky with his thin arms raised, as it seemed to me, imploringly to heaven and protesting by non-resistance against the violence of jungle life. I crept round the thorn bush and fired with a ·303 British army rifle at the aggressor. It was a bad shot ;

there was a flash of yellow fur and the leopard had disappeared into the shadows. But it was force used against force and power against power, and the pacifists on the branch above my head scuttled away in safety. If they had been left to themselves to protect themselves by non-resistance, one at least of them would have died a violent death.

That scene seems to me to contain the parable of pacifism, not, of course, a conclusive argument against the pacifist case, but a parable illustrating a fundamental truth in human history. In the jungle the law is force, violence, power ; non-resistance is of no avail there. Our collateral ancestor, the grey monkey, has remained in the jungle, subject to its law of violence, and for all his non-resistance falling a victim to it. In so far as his near relation man has escaped from the life of the jungle, it has been by resisting force, not by the anarchic individualism of the leopard and the tiger, but by establishing a communal law which forbids the use of force and controls the use of the individual's power and then places communal force as a sanction behind the law.

There is no evidence, as I said, that human beings have yet reached the stage at which non-resistance would be successful against the leopards and the tigers in our midst. On the contrary, everything goes to show that we are still so innately savage and stupid that the communal control of power and force—which means that the community must

enforce the law—is essential if we are to save ourselves from relapse into barbarism. And the first
chapter of this book contains the evidence which
proves that in no sphere of human life is this control
of power and establishment of law more necessary
to-day than in what we call the relations of sovereign
states.

It follows that, if civilization is not to be destroyed
by totalitarian war, human beings must somehow
or other create an international system based upon
law and co-operation, and with international force
as a sanction of international law. But here we
reach an impasse not unusual in human affairs.
Social psychology has not yet reached the stage, as
the history of the League showed, at which there is
any possibility that in a world system the obligations
of collective security will be carried out. Are we,
then, to say with the realist critics of a League system
that it must be for ever utopian, because states will
not treat an act of war against one as an act of war
against all or come to the assistance of the victim of
aggression ?

I believe that the answer to this question is to be
found in common sense, in the ordinary way in
which in ordinary life sensible people continually
deal successfully with such impasses and difficulties.
A goal may be unattainable if you attempt to get to
it in one rush, but may be attainable if you are
prepared to work towards it in stages. This is true
of the international problem. It is possible that at

the end of the war, as we have seen, we may be able to establish limited geographical federal unions, " peace federations ". The federation solves the problem of force so far as the relations of its members are concerned ; it solves it in the non-pacifist way, for the federal or communal power is placed as the sanction behind the federal law. As between the federated states, the armed forces are controlled by the federal government. On the other hand, it was argued above, such limited federations are not by themselves adequate guarantees of world peace or even of continental peace. The relations of states are so closely and so widely articulated that some wider and more universal organization for peace and international co-operation is necessary. Thus while in limited geographical areas federal unions or fully developed international systems of law, co-operation, and collective security may be possible, these limited or regional federations or confederations must be combined in a world system in which collective security is not yet possible.

The solution is to be found perhaps in the distinction between the two series of obligations, vital to an international peace system, referred to on page 215, and in the idea of regionalism within a League system which was put forward by Briand. The world peace system would be a League or confederation of all the states of the world, bound by the first series of obligations which create the method and organization for determining international rules

and laws, for dealing with conflicts of interest, and
for regulating the relations of states on a basis of
compromise and co-operation.   Those obligations
would answer roughly to the League provisions
analysed on pages 100 and 101 under (1), (3), (5), (6),
and (7).   It is worth while to restate them here.   In
the world peace system all states would be bound :

(1)  Under no circumstances to resort to war ;
(2)  To institute a regular procedure of judicial
settlement or of settlement by other pacific methods
and to use this procedure and organization for the
settlement of all disputes or differences which may
arise between them ;
(3)  To disarm ;
(4)  To set up organs and machinery of international
government for carrying out the above provisions
for making international law and for making those
changes in the *status quo* which changing circumstances
from time to time demand, and for promoting the
common interests of states by co-operation.   In
practice that would mean the establishment of an
international court of justice and of organs of a
deliberative or legislative nature, like the League
Council and Assembly.   The experience of the League
showed that, if progress is to be made in the substitution of law for war and co-operation for conflict, and
if provision is really to be made for peaceful change
in the world of states where changing conditions
make it necessary or equitable, the deliberative or
legislative organs of international government must
have the power to make laws or take decisions by
a majority vote.   The *liberum veto* or unanimity rule,
the fetish of the nationalist and of his totem, the
sovereign state, is the negation of all government.

These should be, with one exception, the only

obligations which all states must accept as members of the world peace system. They should not be bound to preserve the independence or territorial integrity of their fellow members against aggression, to treat an act of war against one member as an act of war against all, or to impose " sanctions " against an aggressor. The reason for thus restricting the obligations of states in the world peace system is, as was stated above, psychological. The narrow nationalist psychology is still so strong—and will probably for some time remain so—that there is little chance, in the case of an act of war or aggression, that states all over the world will carry out the obligations of a collective security system demanding immediate, positive, and often dangerous action. It is, however, possible that after the war an important obligation of a less stringent and more negative nature might be accepted and carried out by all the states of the world, namely that they will not aid any state which in any quarter of the world commits an act of aggression or which resorts to war in breach of the fundamental obligations of the peace system.

Within this world peace system, confederation, or commonwealth of nations, which would impose upon its members less stringent or exacting obligations than did the League, there might be regionalized groups and federations of states more closely united by the obligations of collective security. In that case, for instance, the nations of Europe, while each was a member of the world peace system, would collectively be also grouped in a European union or confederation of the kind which Briand proposed. All the states of Europe would be members, it is to be hoped, of this European confederation. It would deal with all international questions which exclusively concerned Europeans and European states and, in order to prevent war in Europe, it would establish a system of collective security for Europe. Its members would therefore be mutually bound to one another by the same obligations as we suggested above for the world peace system, but they would in addition be bound by the obligation to treat an act of war against one as an act of war against all. The European confederation would, therefore, for the affairs of Europe, have its own international organs of government, organs of legislation and of judicial and pacific settlement. It would make European international law and carry through those peaceful changes in the international structure of Europe which must inevitably from time to time become necessary; it would actively promote economic, social and political co-operation in the common interest of all European states. If federal unions were successfully established, e.g. of west European democracies, of the Scandinavian states, or of Danubian states, such federations would enter the European confederation and the world peace system or commonwealth of nations as units.

A European confederation of this kind would exist

within the framework of the world peace system. It would in fact be a regional or continental group of states organized for the purposes of co-operation and peace in so far as, owing to geography and history, they were the exclusive or peculiar concern of that continental group. It might well be that the states in each continent or area would unite in similar regional confederations and that the world peace system would develop through organized relations between these continental confederations rather than through an international organization in which all the states of the world were included as independent units. It is highly probable that it is by a development of this nature that the easiest path to federation, which is no doubt ultimately the most logical and desirable form of international government, may be found.

The realist will, of course, eagerly seize upon the fact that in these suggestions the obligations of a collective security system are proposed for the European confederation, although it was recognized that psychology made them impossible at present in a world confederation. Why, it will be asked, if you admit that collective security proved to be utopian in the League and would again prove utopian in a world confederation, why should you imagine that it would not prove to be utopian in a European confederation ? That is, almost certainly, the form in which the objection would be made and the question asked, and my answer is that the form itself is wrong and actually begs the question. The whole argument of this book is that the realist's use of the word utopian is wrong and it is wrongly used in this question. I do not admit that the League's collective security system was, or that world confederation's collective security system would be, utopian in the sense that there is anything inherent in the nature of states or of their relations, interests, and power which makes such a system impossible. On the contrary, all the evidence goes to prove that such a system is not only possible, but inevitable if the whole fabric of inter-state relations and the civilization which has been built upon it in the last 200 years is not to be destroyed. The collective security system of the League broke down partly because the nationalist psychology of the greater number of the earth's inhabitants made them unwilling to carry out the obligations of the system. I believe that the same psychology would, at the end of the war, again prevent the obligations of collective security being carried out if it was proposed to make it cover all the states of the world. The war will probably have strengthened, rather than weakened, the instinct of say the inhabitants of a South American republic to " keep out of it " where " it " is the anarchic affairs of those barbarous Europeans.

But what applies to the psychology of the Argentinian or Brazilian, when the last bomb in the second European war has been dropped on the last ruined city, does not necessarily apply to the European bar-

barian. Even Mr. Chamberlain and the National Government now see and maintain that we are fighting this war against Hitlerism in defence of an international system of law, order, and co-operation, that it is a war against aggression and to preserve or restore the integrity and independence of small states (which are far away from us and of which we know little), like Czechoslovakia and Norway, and that we are actually by war attempting to establish a collective security system in Europe which the Prime Minister and his colleagues derided as utopian when it might still have been possible to establish it and peace in peace. There is already in these facts some evidence of a not unimportant change in the political psychology of Mr. Chamberlain and people like him. They seem to have reached the stage of admitting that, at any rate within the frontiers of Europe, the old system of power politics, conflict, and totalitarian war must somehow or other be brought to an end, that a new system of law and co-operation must take its place, and that the power of the law-abiding and pacific states must be used collectively to maintain international law and safeguard the security of each and all.

This change in those who were most impervious to the political psychology without which no stable organization of international peace in Europe can be created is some evidence that they have learnt by experience. Our scientists with infinite patience

and solemnity have proved for us that the earthworm, the liver fluke, and the flea learn by experience and that the dog can be taught to salivate in
the mouth when his master rings a bell.   There are
therefore no real grounds for despairing eternally
of British Prime Ministers and other human inhabitants of the European continent.   It is not true that
they or the rest of the human race are incapable of
doing politically what the earthworm and the dog
have done in other spheres of life.   There is no
conclusive scientific evidence yet for assuming that
the capacity of learning by experience in human
beings is strictly confined to burnt children.   On the
contrary there were clear signs, as we saw in the first
chapter, that at the end of the  1914  war large
numbers of Europeans had begun to learn by that
experience, that their psychology had changed and
that they were prepared for and even demanded a
change in the international system from power and
conflict to law, co-operation, and collective security.
It is true that they had not learnt their lesson
thoroughly enough and the change in their psychology was too superficial and unstable to save
them from the horrors of a second totalitarian war.
But that is no reason for assuming that at the end of
this second war accumulated experience may not
induce them to learn the lesson a little better and
that the change in psychology may not this time be
deeper and more stable.   A child sometimes has to
burn itself twice before it learns to fear the fire and

even Pavlov's salivating dog, who is now held up to us as the model for all human psychology, has to hear the bell ring more than once before his mouth learns to water.

We Europeans have heard the bell of totalitarian warfare tolling twice in a generation all over our continent. If the dog learnt that food in the shape of raw meat was inevitably connected with the ringing of Pavlov's bell, we have learnt that unredeemed misery and barbarism are inevitably connected with an international system of power politics, conflict, and war. From the point of view merely of political and social organization, the machinery of international government, there is, as I have frequently insisted in this book, no mystery or insuperable difficulty. Our long and bitter experience of government in human communities, ranging over several thousand years, leaves no doubt what in broad outline is the system of interstate or international government which we must set up in Europe if we intend to make totalitarian war improbable instead of inevitable by basing the relations of states upon law and co-operation and collective security. The question is whether the experience of two wars will have left Europeans with the international psychology, the sense of a common danger from war and a unity of interest in peace, without which the collective security system cannot function. I do not say that it will. But the European will have passed through an experience which has not been shared by the rest of the world. Many people, besides our Prime Ministers, may have revised their opinions with regard to what is or is not utopian after this second war. That is why, although one may doubt whether the rest of the world, e.g. the Brazilian or the Argentinian, will have suffered the psychological change necessary for a world collective security system, it is possible that the psychology of the European will have changed sufficiently to make such a system feasible in Europe.

It is possible. No student of human history will say more than that. But there is one categorical prophecy which he can make with some assurance. If some such system as that outlined in these pages is not established—providing for the rule of international law and co-operation, control of national power, and collective defence against international aggression—there are only two alternatives before Europe. The continued existence of the closely articulated international society in which we are actually living is incompatible with the anarchic system of sovereign, autarkic states pursuing their " national interests " by power politics, conflict, and war. If the system continues, the society will be destroyed. The process has already begun, for the destruction of our society means the destruction of our civilization as it developed in the nineteenth century and a regression to pre-industrial society. But there is another alternative which very few people in democratic countries contemplate, but which is not improbable. If we refuse to create the international organization and government which the form of our society demands, the destruction of this closely articulated, industrialized, international society may not follow, but it may itself impose upon us, willy nilly, a political organization in which it can continue to function. In other words, the federation or confederation of Europe and the world, which is the political organization demanded by the economic and social organization of Europe and the world, if it is not consciously achieved by the democratic methods of co-operation and law agreed to by the several national communities, may be imposed by force of arms and authoritarian conquest. That is the only vital principle in the Nazi, Fascist, and Stalinist dictatorships which have sprung up in the last few years. If the international government which our society demands is not established on a democratic and socialist basis by free national communities, it may be established in the form of slave empires by dictators.

CHAPTER IV

A NOTE ON REASON

In the previous chapter I have dealt with three out
of the four main objections to an international peace
system on the model of the League which were stated
on pages 107–8. The fourth or remaining objection
is concerned with what is known as the problem
of " peaceful change ". It is maintained that a
League system which attempts to base international
relations upon international law and obligations
created by treaties must inevitably pin international
society eternally in the straight-jacket of the *status quo*.
No matter what happens in the world to change the
actual relations of states and peoples, their internal
or external economic or demographic needs or
circumstances, it will be impossible to change the
structure of international society or the laws and
obligations which maintain it in its old form, if it is
in the interest of any nation to prevent such a change.
For the case of any state whose interests demand such
a change is already judged against it by the fact
that the " rights " of the state which resists the change
are protected by existing law or treaty. Take for
instance the case of the Sudeten Germans or of the

232

## A Note on Reason

Italian nationals in Tunis. It is not necessary here to determine whether the German and Italian contentions are or are not justified ; it is, however, obvious that they may be, i.e. that facts and justice demand an alteration in the frontier or in the status and rights of certain inhabitants of a state. But the League provided no effective method of making such a change peacefully, no matter how just or desirable or necessary it might be. It would be useless for Germany or Italy in such a case to bring the matter before the League, for the rights and obligations which created the existing situation were determined by international law and treaties, and the law and treaties were an impregnable defence for the state resisting change. For Germany and Italy were in effect demanding a change in the law or a revocation of treaty rights, and the system itself made this impossible without the consent of the other side whose interest it was to resist any change. The League therefore made the *status quo* unalterable except by violence or war.

There is no doubt—and it has already been admitted in these pages—that this criticism draws attention to a serious defect in the League system. So far it is justified. But the conclusion which the critics seek to draw—that no international system of this kind is possible because it cannot provide for peaceful change—is nonsense. The same argument could be used against all government or communal organization based upon law. It is true that law

is always upon the side of the *status quo* and that it
is therefore upon the side of those whose interest it
is to keep things as they are. But that has not
prevented human beings from developing social
systems which are based upon law and which at the
same time provide methods and organization for
changing the law and the social *status quo*. Those
who tell us that this or that is " impossible " in
international government continually assume that
the human race has no experience in the problems
of government and the ordering of their society,
that the problem of establishing law and preventing
violence and conflict in the relations between
national communities is *sui generis*, and that we can
therefore find nothing relevant in past history which
can help us to solve it. This is another example
of our inveterate habit of divorcing politics from
common sense. On the contrary, we know in broad
outline, from our long experience of human society
and government, exactly what we have to do if we
want to combine a system of law, order, and co-
operation with progress and change in the law itself
and in the fundamental relations within the system.
Every club, society, or trade union ; every village
commune or urban municipality ; every national
constitution or federation has been " faced " with
the same problem. And over and over again the
problem has been solved, sometimes more, and
sometimes less successfully. It has been solved by
the common-sense method of incorporating within

## A Note on Reason

your system of government regular organs and procedure for making changes and altering laws. There is no evidence of any kind that there is anything in national communities and states which makes it impossible to introduce successfully into an international system based upon law and collective security similar methods, organs, and procedure for altering the law and making radical changes in the relations of national communities. It is true that those who framed its Covenant failed to do this effectively. It is not my purpose in this book to suggest in detail the structure of the international peace system which might be set up at the end of the war.[1] My object is to see whether one can draw the broad outlines of an international system of law, co-operation, and peace, using for the purpose simply common sense and our experience of human government, and then to discover whether there is any reason for believing those who tell us that to attempt to establish such a system after the war is utopian and impossible. I do not therefore propose to describe the organs or procedure which might be established for making international law and effecting peaceful change. But here again common sense and experience enables one to state with certainty what the general outline of this part of the inter-

---

[1] I did this twenty-five years ago during the first totalitarian war in a book called *International Government* and time does not seem to me to have invalidated its main conclusions. This of course may be due to mental sclerosis, to which we are all liable, but on the other hand it may possibly be due to the fact that the conclusions were right.

national system must be if Europeans wish to avoid totalitarian war in the future. Somewhere in the international organization there must be an organ of a legislative nature with power to make effective decisions both regarding the making of laws or rules, the revision of treaties, and demands for fundamental changes.

I have now reached the end of the strictly limited task which I set myself in this book. There are other conditions of the first importance which will have to be fulfilled if law and co-operation are to be substituted for power and war as the determining factors in the relations of European states and the fate of Europeans. For the reason given in the preceding paragraph I have not dealt with them and do not propose to deal with them, for they are concerned with the detailed working rather than with broad structural outlines of the international system. There is, however, one question of such importance that it must at least be mentioned. No one can doubt that Europeans have involved themselves, and with themselves the whole human race, in one of the great crises of history and civilization. Anyone who was a young man at the beginning of this century will remember that at that time the future seemed to contain a real possibility of greater prosperity and happiness, of a wider and deeper civilization, for human beings than had ever existed in their previous history. Many people believed and still more hoped that the possibility would be

## A Note on Reason

fulfilled. Neither the belief nor the hope was unreasonable, for in fact all these things were easily within our reach. To-day the future of the race is darker and more threatening than it has been in a thousand years of history. Historical changes or events of this magnitude are not due to any single cause or series of causes, but among the factors which have produced this terrible reversal of fortune it is possible to say with absolute certainty that one has had a particularly devastating effect. That factor is the international system, as we call it, which means simply the methods by which we have chosen to regulate the political, economic, and social relations of states, or rather of the individual men and women organized in these states or national communities. The Hitlers, Mussolinis, Stalins, Francos, Chamberlains, Hoares, Lavals, and Bonnets, the doctrines and practice of fascism and communism, the betrayal of democracy by democrats—all these things and persons, no doubt, have had their effect. But the persons at any rate are mere puppet shadows projected upon the screen of history by causes infinitely more powerful than themselves. The most potent of these causes is the international system.

In the previous pages, when considering the international system and its disintegrating effects upon European society, I have more than once had to insist that this disintegrating effect has been largely due to the fact that the system is a contradiction in social terms. European society is economically and socially an international society. That is not a statement about sociological, economic, or political theory ; it is a statement about facts, about the lives that you and I and everyone else lived and live in the industrialized Europe which came into existence during the last century. Economically, and to a large extent socially, we live international lives. Yet we have consistently refused to recognize the fact in the international system, the political and economic organization of international relations. Every year for the last hundred years the lives we led have demanded more and more international co-operation and closer economic and political articulation of national communities, and every year almost, under the lethal influence of nationalist psychology and the anachronistic belief in the " inevitability " and " reality " of the conflict of " national interests ",[1] we have made the organiza-

[1] I was about to add " the competitive psychology of capitalism ", but have deliberately refrained. The psychology of conflicting national interests is itself a particular instance of the disintegrating competitive psychology of capitalism. I believe that capitalism has played a tremendous part in creating the international anarchy of to-day. But I have purposely excluded a discussion of this. The subject of this book is, I repeat, the form which international government—the organization of the relations of national communities—must take if law and co-operation are to take the place of power and war. Whether the national communities have a socialist or capitalist internal organization does not affect this problem. If the inter-state relations of socialist states are based on power and conflict, the results will be exactly the same as in the case of capitalist states, as the war of the Soviet Union upon Finland shows, and if all the states in the world were socialist, the problem which this book discusses would remain : how should the relations between these states be regulated if we want to prevent national conflict or war ?

238

tion itself nationally one of ever-increasing political and economic isolation and internationally one of ever-increasing political and economic conflict.

The nemesis of complete imbecility is not confined to individual imbeciles. A society which lives in one way and secretes a political and social organization which makes that kind of life impossible, which in fact makes possible only an exactly opposite kind of life, will suffer inevitably the nemesis of social disruption. That is what is happening, and why it is happening, in the international society of Europeans. These considerations lead to an important conclusion with regard to the world after the war. It is not true that the League system, as established after the other war, did nothing in the economic sphere ; it performed some important and many highly useful functions. But the causes which led to its political failure and which have been analysed in this book denied it the power decisively to affect international economic relations. If a second attempt is made to establish a peace system in Europe, we must learn from that experience. To set up the political framework necessary for law and co-operation is not in itself enough. Whether the international organization is a federation, a confederation, or a League, or a combination of all three, it is essential that it should immediately apply itself to the task of promoting the common international economic interests, of developing the international

economic and social services that the lives which we
Europeans actually live cry aloud for. Here again
I do not propose to suggest or discuss the details of
a possible programme of action. But one thing is
obvious. If the economic reconstruction of a
devastated Europe can be accomplished, it will
require common action by all the peoples of Europe,
whether they were enemies, allies, or neutrals in the
war. Here is a field in which a new peace system,
rising out of the ashes of the war and the grave of
the League, might well lay the foundations of
permanent economic co-operation between the
nations and peoples of Europe.

This brings me to a final point. I have never yet
written a book about history or politics without
some critic sooner or later writing : " Mr. Woolf
seems to think that people act more rationally than
they do ", or " Mr. Woolf seems to be quite wrong
in believing that people are politically rational." I
have no doubt that someone will sooner or later say
the same about this book. It is only when writers
are very young that they delude themselves with the
hope that they can make their meaning clear or
that people will even take the trouble to understand
what they are trying to say. It is many years since
I have suffered from that delusion. Yet even now
it seems to me inexplicable that anyone, looking
round the world to-day, can believe that human
beings are influenced to any great extent by reason
in their political actions or can imagine that anyone

else believes it. The author of this book does not believe and never has believed it.

But that is really not the final word on the matter. The fact that human beings are not to any great extent influenced by reason in political action does not mean that their social actions always are and always must be irrational nor that it is the duty of the historian or publicist merely to rationalize the stupidity and savagery of man, to try to prove by reason that we are quite right to act irrationally. The historian and writer on politics ought, in my view, to be the humblest of scientists ; he ought to try, in so far as it is possible, to analyse the nature and effects of the psychology and acts of human beings in communities. In order to do that he must, like every other scientist, use reason. It may be admitted that the individual and communal actions of the amœba or earthworm are not to any great extent determined by reason, but no one thinks that the scientist who studies their habits should therefore discard reason in his investigations and himself adopt as the only apparatus of investigation the psychology of a unicellular organism or a worm. His study of these creatures may even enable him by the use of reason or common sense to predict with considerable certainty that if a worm acts in one way, one series of events will follow, but that if he acts in another way, another series of events will follow. The fact that he can and does make the prediction does not, however, imply that he

241

believes that worms will in future act rationally on this knowledge.

I confess to believing that human beings are slightly more rational than the amœba and the worm. Their actions are occasionally determined by reason or common sense. If a man comes to me and says : " I want to get to-day from Lewes to London by 10 o'clock ", I can tell him with comparative certainty what he must do in order to achieve this. In doing so, I shall undoubtedly be using reason and so will he. I shall tell him that if he does X, Y will follow, and if he does A, B will follow. If he tells me that he wants to be in London at 10 o'clock and also in Eastbourne at 9.55, I can tell him with absolute certainty that he is wanting to do two things which are incompatible and that he must choose either the one or the other. All this is " using one's reason " and in such circumstances the man will nine times out of ten be convinced and " act accordingly ".

Take another simple case. Suppose a man comes to me in May and says : " I have a garden of about half an acre and I want to grow in it next year a certain number of flowers and also the maximum quantity of vegetables ; I don't like parsnips, but I want a very large number of broccoli. Can you tell me the best way of doing this ? " I can. I can give him a detailed plan of what his garden should be all through the following twelve months if he wants to get the maximum amount of vegetables all through the year, with no parsnips but quite a lot of broccoli, and a certain number of flowers. I will tell him exactly where and when and what amount to sow all through the year. And I can predict, with absolute certainty, that if he wants X, say peas in the summer of next year, he must do Y, namely sow peas in a certain way and place at intervals from March to June. I can also tell him with absolute certainty that certain things in gardening are incompatible ; that, for instance, he cannot grow peas and runner beans in the same row, and that if he tries to do so, he will get neither. Observe that I do not say to him : "If you do X, Y will inevitably follow", but only : "If you want Y to happen, you must do X" ; for instance, if he wants peas in the summer he must sow them between March and June, but that does not mean that he will get his peas ; mice or birds may eat them or storms destroy them or mildew wither them ; but it still remains true—and the truth is not unimportant —that if he wants peas in the summer, he must sow them between March and June.

All this knowledge and the action which follows it are based to quite a considerable extent upon the use of reason or common sense, which is reason applied to experience. There is not the slightest ground for believing that similarly reason cannot be applied or that it never is applied to experience in politics and society. The object of this book is to treat the problem of war in the same way as that

243

in which we treat the problem of getting from Lewes to London or of plotting out one's garden for the growing of vegetables. The problem is infinitely more complicated, but it can only be solved in the same way, by applying reason to experience. If the problem is approached in this common-sense way, it is possible to predict that, if Europeans want peace, they must do certain things, and that if they do certain other things, they will get Hitlers and totalitarian war. And what applies to peas applies to peace. Using reason, we can tell a man what he must do if he wants peas, but that does not imply that we believe that he will use *his* reason and get peas. We have sufficient experience of society and government to be able in the year 1940, by using our reason on this experience, to tell Europeans what they must do if they want peace, but that does not mean that we believe that they will use *their* reason, do it, or obtain peace.